The Principal's Guide to

Raising Reading Achievement

The
Principal's
Guide to

Raising
Reading
Achievement

Elaine K. McEwan

CORWIN PRESS, INC.
A Sage Publications Company
Thousand Oaks, California

For information:

Corwin Press, Inc.
A Sage Publications Company
2455 Teller Road
Thousand Oaks, California 91320
E-mail: order@corwinpress.com

SAGE Publications Ltd.
6 Bonhill Street
London EC2A 4PU
United Kingdom

SAGE Publications India Pvt. Ltd.
M-32 Market
Greater Kailash I
New Delhi 110 048 India

Printed in the United States of America

Library of Congress Cataloging-in-Publication Data

McEwan, Elaine K., 1941-
    The principal's guide to raising reading achievement / Elaine K. McEwan.
        p.   cm.
    Includes bibliographical references and index.
    ISBN 0-8039-6627-X (cloth : acid-free paper). — ISBN 0-8039-6628-8 (pbk. : acid-free paper)
    1. Reading (Elementary).   2. Elementary school principals. I. Title.
LB1573.M1664   1997
372.41—dc21
                                                                98-8874

This book is printed on acid-free paper.

98 99 00 01 02 03   10 9 8 7 6 5 4 3 2 1

Production Editor: S. Marlene Head
Editorial Assistant: Julia Parnell
Typesetter: Andrea D. Swanson
Indexer: Teri Davis Greenberg
Cover Designer: Marcia M. Rosenburg

Contents

About the Author

Elaine K. McEwan is an educational consultant with the McEwan-Adkins Group, which offers training in leadership and team building, raising reading achievement, and parent-community issues. A former teacher, librarian, principal, and assistant superintendent for instruction in a suburban Chicago school district, she is the author of more than two dozen books including titles for parents and teachers (*Attention Deficit Disorder*), fiction for middle-grade students (*Joshua McIntire Series*), and guides for administrators (*Leading Your Team to Excellence: How to Make Quality Decisions; The Principal's Guide to Attention Deficit Hyperactivity Disorder; How to Deal With Parents Who Are Angry, Frightened, Troubled, or Just Plain Crazy;* and *Seven Steps to Effective Instructional Leadership*). She is the education columnist for the *Oro Valley Explorer* (Arizona) newspaper, is a contributing editor to several parenting magazines on educational issues, and can be heard on a variety of syndicated radio programs helping parents solve schooling problems. She was honored by the Illinois Principals Association as an outstanding instructional leader, by the Illinois State Board of Education with an Award of Excellence in the Those Who Excel Program, and by the National Association of Elementary School Principals as the National Distinguished Principal from Illinois for 1991. She received her undergraduate degree in education from Wheaton College and graduate degrees in library science and educational administration from Northern Illinois University. McEwan lives with her husband and business partner, E. Raymond Adkins, in Oro Valley, Arizona.

Introduction

Reading has always been my passion. As a child growing up in rural Michigan, I filled the lazy days of summer with reading. I bicycled weekly from my home to the behemoth bookmobile, rusty and dusty but filled with adventures, and I checked out as many volumes as my wire basket would safely hold. Parked in the same vacant lot each week, the bookmobile held excitement and the opportunity to travel to places I was sure I'd never go. I made friends with the librarian and she brought my favorites each week—mysteries and horse stories. Even the frightening barking dogs that ran from long driveways to snap at my heels as I furiously pedaled by did not deter me from my mission. I craved books. I still do. I'm a regular at the libraries in Tucson, Arizona, where I live, "schlepping" home sackloads of books to fire my imagination and assist me in my research and writing. Rather than thumbing well-worn cards in the catalog to find choice treasures, I now access the collections from my personal computer. But the thrill of reading is still there.

That passion has fueled my professional life as well. As a classroom teacher, learning-center teacher/librarian, elementary school principal, and finally as assistant superintendent for instruction, I was relentless in my pursuit of reading proficiency for all students, but especially for those who came to school without the background and readiness to read: those students who spoke another language, were poor and hungry, or whose hours were filled with violent TV rather than nursery rhymes and picture books.

In 1983 I became an elementary principal in a small K-8 district in the suburbs of Chicago. Although the district was home to affluent areas where the horsey set built sprawling estates and upwardly mobile young executives moved their growing families into its burgeoning subdivisions, my K-6 school fronted on railroad tracks in the central downtown. The building was old, the playground was rusty, and the fading, peeling paint in the hallways was a fitting backdrop for a demoralized veteran faculty. The standardized test scores of their students were abysmal and they were feeling increasing pressure at their inability to make a difference. They had plenty of explanations (excuses) for this sad state of affairs:

- Nearly half of the student population was Hispanic.
- Many students came from migrant families.

- There was little parental support.
- Over half of the students were on free and reduced lunch.
- Many students came from single-parent families.
- The student turnover was close to 30%.
- All decisions regarding curriculum and budget were made by the central office.

In the 8 years I served as building principal, student achievement rose dramatically, parental involvement as measured by PTA membership and financial support tripled, and our image in the community was reversed. Our sixth-grade Battle of the Books team won the city championship more than once, defeating teams from more affluent schools as well as the private school in town.

How did we reach our goals? Study, research, experimentation, and risk taking. Teachers participated in planning and decision making through a building leadership team. The faculty came to view their principal as an instructional leader rather than a manager. Decisions were no longer made unilaterally; the group participated and was held accountable. Rather than following recipes and rules that were no longer working, we hypothesized and tested new ideas. We focused on outcomes rather than textbooks, and expectations moved from a belief that "some can learn" to the belief that "all can learn."

The critical issues surrounding reading achievement and instruction in this country are now debated in the popular press. The evidence of reading difficulty in studies like the National Assessment of Educational Progress (NAEP) is hard to ignore. Who is responsible for changing this disturbing trend? We are. As instructional leaders of our schools, we must make a difference, one school at a time.

I have written *The Principal's Guide to Raising Reading Achievement* with these goals in mind: (a) to convince you of the power that rests in you and your faculty to create a "school of readers," (b) to introduce you to the most current research in reading instruction so that you and your faculty can make informed decisions, and (c) to share with you the eight key components you need to achieve your goals.

Chapter 1 explores some of the reasons why students can't read and suggests that you and your faculty focus only on those things you can change. Chapter 2 summarizes the running debate between proponents of phonics and whole language and helps you understand why reading instruction cannot be an "either-or" proposition. Chapter 3 describes the eight key components that need to be in place to create a school of readers. Chapter 4 sets forth the essential learnings that need to occur at each instructional level, and Chapter 5 covers the topic of remedial reading and what you can do to help the at-risk and learning disabled child. Chapter 6 contains 30+ things you can do tomorrow to raise reading achievement in your school. At the end of the book are many useful resources with practical information you can use immediately.

Although there are dangers inherent in separating reading instruction from the broad umbrella of language arts (and I would certainly never do it in the context of instruction), I have not specifically included the skills of writing, spelling, and speaking in my discussion here. Their omission does not reflect my feelings regarding their importance and the close relationship they bear to the teaching of reading, but rather the constraints of time and space. Another word of warning: I have not spared the reference citations to research studies in this book. I don't want you take just my word for the advice I'm giving. It is based on the collective research and writing of hundreds of scholars.

When I first opened the file containing the 1983 standardized test scores for my school, I wanted to cry. More than half of the students were reading below grade level, some of them appallingly so. This same scenario is repeated yearly at thousands of schools across the country and it doesn't have to be. Ron Edmonds (1981) said before his untimely death in 1983:

> We can, whenever and wherever we choose, successfully teach all children whose schooling is of interest to us. We already know more than we need to do that. Whether or not we do it must finally depend on how we feel about the fact that we haven't so far. (p. 53)

Although Edmonds was speaking in the broad sense about student achievement, his statement could well be paraphrased to focus solely on reading.

We can, whenever and wherever we choose, successfully teach all children to read. We already have reams of research, hundreds of successful programs, and thousands of effective schools to show us the way. Whether or not we do it must finally depend on how we feel about the fact that we haven't so far.

1

Why Our Kids
Aren't Learning to Read

Have you ever rightly considered what the mere ability to read means? That it is the key which admits us to the whole world of thought and fancy and imagination? To the company of saint and sage, of the wisest and the wittiest at their wisest and wittiest moment? That it enables us to see with the keenest eyes, hear with the finest ears, and listen to the sweetest voice of all times?

James Russell Lowell (1871, p. 9)

*I*t's that time of year again—your school's test scores are about to be released to the newspaper. Reading achievement has dropped for the third straight time. You're dreading the telephone calls, questions, and finger-pointing. Your palms are already sweaty at the prospect of a confrontational meeting with parents and reporters. The board of education is expecting a report next week. Faced with the terrifyingly abysmal performance of your students, you are scrambling for some explanations or reasons. You'd even be happy if you could place the blame squarely on someone else's shoulders.

You're not alone in the sinking ship in which you find yourself. The trend respects no geographic area. From "sea to shining sea" kids aren't learning to read. In Maryland, two thirds of third graders aren't meeting the state's standards for reading (Athans, 1997). Reading achievement in Illinois (in the three grades tested) has declined steadily over the past 5 years (Rossi, 1997). California's fourth-grade students came in last in a national ranking of the 39 states that participated in the 1994 National Assessment of Educational Progress (NAEP) (Office of Educational Research and Improvement, 1996).

You and your teachers are dedicated, well meaning, and hardworking. Why aren't you achieving the results you so desperately want? Figuring out the precise reasons for your school's reading problem may well be as challenging and elusive as solving this week's *New York Times* crossword. But be patient. There are answers ahead.

All the stakeholders in the educational game have their own set of excuses, reasons, explanations, or even accusations regarding the reading crisis. Before we look at what you as an instructional leader can do in your school to reverse the downward trend, let's examine the issue from several different perspectives.

The Insiders' Perspective: Excuses and Explanations From the Trenches

A variety of reasons (some call them excuses) are offered by "insiders" (administrators and teachers) regarding why the students in their schools or systems do poorly on standardized tests, leading most of us to conclude that these young people haven't learned to read at all or at least they can't read at grade level. Please do not think I'm suggesting that the variables embedded in the following excuses such as socioeconomic status, student ability, class size, finance, school governance, and parental involvement are not genuine issues. What I am suggesting, however, is that to see them as insurmountable barriers is inexcusable. You can go around, through, and over these problems. Successful principals across the country are doing it. In addition to the excuses, I'll offer some ideas for you to think about as you determine for yourself why your students aren't learning to read.

Students aren't ready to learn. Lack of reading readiness is one of the most frequently used reasons to explain reading failure. When children come to school without sufficient exposure to books and language, they have a lot of catching up to do, and many of these students never manage to make it out of the starting gate. Sometimes they're placed in "developmental programs," where they'll have the time they need to mature, or are referred to remedial reading or special education. Others are retained to repeat one or more grades in school or are socially promoted. But in spite of all of our interventions, a large percentage of these kids fall through the cracks and are lost forever. Even those who manage to learn to read (albeit much later than in first grade) are so far behind their age-mates by the time they reach middle or high school, they soon start counting the days until they can drop out or become the proverbial troublemakers and class clowns.

Something to Think About: In spite of the billions we have spent on Head Start, early intervention, at-risk programs, special education, and Title I, many educators do not seem to be gaining on the problem, causing them to feel powerless in the face of such odds. Many schools, however, are overcoming the sometimes overwhelming odds of failure. We must look at schools and programs where educators are achieving success and learn from them.

Parents are to blame. Another variation on the "students aren't ready" theme is this often-repeated excuse: "Parents aren't doing enough." They aren't educated. They don't care. They don't provide enough discipline. They don't spend enough time with their children. In response to plummeting reading scores on the Illinois Goal Assessment Program (IGAP) (Rossi, 1997), State Superintendent Joseph

Spagnolo (1997) sent a letter to newspapers around the state suggesting that parents spend more time reading at home with their children.

"Illinois reading scores statewide have dropped steadily in the last five years," he wrote. "That news, unwelcome as it is, should ring alarm bells for anyone concerned about the education of our young people." He goes on to suggest that "it's up to parents to fill the pages of their children's lives with meaningful, productive and useful skills and experiences" (Spagnolo, 1997, p. 17). Although the superintendent was subtle in his missive, the message was unmistakable: Parents, you have to do more. If you were doing a better job, we wouldn't be in such a pickle. Unfortunately, parents don't take too kindly to being blamed for something they see as the school's responsibility.

Something to Think About: James Coleman (1966) in a massive education research project funded by the federal government shocked educators when he reported that differences in the resources of schools were not that important. Rather, it was the background of students that made the difference. His report, which set in motion the large-scale busing plans of the late 1960s so that blacks could sit next to whites in schools, completely overlooked instructional leadership, curriculum, and teaching effectiveness as variables that just might affect student achievement. In response to Coleman's indictment of schools, a group of researchers began to focus on school effectiveness, showing that the following variables clearly made an impact on student achievement: administrative leadership, climate conducive to learning, schoolwide emphasis on learning, teacher expectations of achievement, monitoring system of pupil progress tied to instructional objectives, parent involvement, and time on task (Edmonds, 1979; Purkey & Smith, 1983; Rutter, Maughan, Mortimore, & Ouston, 1979).

I was just following orders. This excuse says in so many words: "I can't be faulted for the poor performance of my students because I didn't have any input into the decision about which methods, materials, or programs I had to use." This "pass the buck" move is convenient when you're part of a state or district where someone else dictates curriculum to you. Administrators and teachers in the state of California were given no choice in 1988 when the State Board of Education dictated that a literature-based approach to the teaching of reading would be the order of the day. Although the words *whole language* did not appear in the directive, the implication seemed clear enough to the practitioners particularly when no programs with explicit phonics were included in the approved materials list. The disastrous showing of California's students on the 1994 NAEP set in motion a juggernaut of finger-pointing, blame, and political maneuvering (Lemann, 1997). At least one person involved in that decision has apologized and is now on the road to reform the way reading is currently being taught in California. Former state superintendent Bill Honig has publicly apologized for his role, written a book (1996), and formed a foundation to right the wrongs he set in motion (Coalition on Reading, or CORE).

Something to Think About: Before we implemented a program that gave building-based leadership teams both authority and accountability, the teachers spent a lot of time blaming central office and/or the board of education for their problems. Getting control of both the budget and the curriculum was pretty scary at first because now we couldn't blame anyone else if we failed. Autonomy gave us the freedom to choose the curriculum, methodologies, and grouping practices that fit our student population.

Class sizes are too large. The class size research is widely debated and discussed, especially by boards of education trying to make decisions about budget cuts and by older community members who remember learning to read just fine in classes of 40+ students. There is a point of no return, however, when overloaded classes affect the quality of instruction unfavorably, but that usually occurs when teachers and administrators give up. Many whole-language proponents in the California reading wars are pointing to the overloaded classes during the period of time under consideration as a reason for the current dismal reading achievement (Routman, 1996, p. 21).

Something to Think About: This is a "fuzzy" excuse that is difficult to document, but any administrator who's been there knows that teachers with classes of over 30 students have poor morale, lower self-esteem, and use more sick days. Don't feed this malaise, however, by giving your teachers permission to blame big classes. Find ways to support them and share the burden.

We don't have enough money. Lack of funding for public education is always a marvelous scapegoat. There's never enough of the pie to go around and what there is may frequently be distributed inequitably. This inequity only serves to widen the gap between the "haves" and the "have-nots" and gives those of us who serve in schools with less to spend per pupil the perfect out for poor performance. Ken Goodman (1995) in a critique of the Report of the California Task Force on Reading charged that "many of those whom the schools are failing are in unsafe buildings taught by uncertified teachers." He went on to say that "since Proposition 13, California spends less per-pupil than almost all other industrialized states" (p. 39). The excuse is: How can we accomplish anything when we aren't spending as much per pupil as more affluent states/districts/schools?

Something to Think About: I personally have never found that lack of money was a stumbling block to doing something that I really wanted to do to improve instruction (at the local school level). The district in which I worked spent less than the state average per pupil expenditure, so money was always in short supply. But I sought out several local businesses who employed many of our parents. Through school-business partnerships I always found the money I needed. There are hundreds of private schools with top-notch reading scores that often operate within old substandard buildings, without technology or modern equipment.

There are too many students with learning and physical disabilities, ADHD, and behavioral disorders. The recent trend in many districts of including students with disabilities in the regular classroom has many educators feeling frustrated with their multiple roles. They ask (and sometimes even whine): "How can I do an adequate job of teaching reading if I have to teach students with Down's syndrome, autism, and severe learning and behavior disorders?"

Something to Think About: Students with disabilities often come with instructional aides and facilitators. Use these resources to help all of the students in your classrooms. If these resources don't seem to be available, become an active participant in the IEP process to ensure that students with more involved disabilities are properly supported in the regular classroom.

The tests used to measure reading achievement are poorly constructed and multiple-choice items don't fairly measure critical thinking skills. When students don't do as well as expected on a test, one way to explain away the results is to attack the tests. In Illinois where the state-required IGAP is administered yearly in March to 6th, 8th, and 10th graders, the 5-year record shows a steady decline. Scores on the 500-point reading test are down an average of 38 points since 1993, and at 10th grade the loss is 42 points. The response of some educators in the state to this dismal news was to question the validity of the test. Critics charged that the passages were too long, students were required to choose as many as three correct answers rather than the typical one answer required on the usual standardized test, and there was an undue emphasis on details and trivial information (Rossi, 1997).

In the affluent Fox Valley area of Illinois, suburban St. Charles School District implemented curricular changes that even their early literature described as "pathbreaking" and "revolutionary." There's been only one problem: The students' test scores keep dropping. District administrators have explained to parents that the IGAP and achievement tests don't test the critical thinking skills students are being taught and that they are planning to implement a full-scale battery of performance assessments (M. Damer, personal communication, November 6, 1997).

Something to Think About: Blaming the tests is like "shooting the messenger," and I happen to think educators look pretty silly when they overdo this excuse. Interestingly enough, on the California Bar Exam, the largest program so far to have incorporated performance testing, the rank order of applicants is almost the same on the performance, essay, and multiple-choice sections. Low-scoring students score low on all three parts; high-scoring candidates score high on all three. The same thing has happened on the free-response and multiple-choice parts of the Advanced Placement computer science exam (Feinberg, 1990).

Standardized tests don't really assess a true range of literacy skills. Proponents of the whole-language philosophy often blame low test scores on the fact that standardized tests can't really do an adequate job of assessing the full range of a child's abilities to make sense of written language. If a student doesn't do well on a standardized test, it's not because he can't read, they propose. It's just because the test is not measuring his skills in a comparable way to which he was taught or that educators haven't given the student enough time to "integrate all available information in authentic literacy events" (Goodman, 1993, p. 108).

Something to Think About: Translated, I think that means that a child in second grade shouldn't necessarily be expected to pass a second-grade standardized test. He's just not ready yet. Does this *really* make sense to you?

The students speak another language. A heavy concentration of what educators call bilingual students (a misnomer because if these students were really bilingual they wouldn't be having problems with English) is a widely used excuse for low scores. Ken Goodman, chief proponent of the whole-language philosophy of instruction, shifted the entire blame for California's low reading scores on the NAEP to minority students. "The real story in California is that the state is still doing a bad job of educating minority kids" (Libit & Bowler, 1997). Goodman further points out that all of the states and territories that ranked low on the NAEP have a wide diversity of income and/or ethnicity (Goodman, 1995, p. 39).

Something to Think About: Bilingual education is a political minefield, and as someone who has experienced it firsthand, I find a lot not to like about the way it's done. Conventional wisdom in this field calls for teaching a child to read in his or her primary language first and then transitioning the child to reading in English. I found this to be an especially nonsensical plan for those Spanish-speaking children who were born in this country and whose older siblings had attended public schools. These children may "speak" Spanish, but by virtue of their immersion in American culture and TV since birth, they already "read" and "understand" a great deal of English. In my opinion, these children should be enrolled in all-English preschools and kindergartens where they will flourish and soon be on grade level with their peers. Many of our parents were savvy enough to insist on doing this, and although we were not permitted to openly encourage parents, we certainly shared the option with them.

We don't have enough time. There's no question that the schools are being asked to do far more today than they ever were. Sex and drug education, economic education, conflict resolution, and environmental awareness are just a few of the trendy topics that have made their way into most curriculum guides. The problem is that educators don't have a longer school day or year so we're doing more with less. So, if we're not doing a good job in some area, we can always plead lack of time and an overloaded curriculum.

Something to Think About: Whatever happened to setting priorities? Give your teachers permission to focus on what's really important. Students listening to DARE lectures aren't developing their reading skills.

We're constantly being asked to do new things without a chance to perfect and evaluate what we were doing last year. "Been there, done that." "What goes around comes around." "This too shall pass." We are our own worst enemies in education as we move with excitement to embrace a new program or methodology (sometimes without considering either the research or the ramifications). We want to be "up-to-date," "on the cutting edge," and "innovative," but we're often setting ourselves up to fail.

Something to Think About: Beware of trying to do too much at once. Overloading teachers with new programs not only wears them out but makes it impossible to do a competent evaluation. When evaluating a program for possible implementation ask these questions: (a) Is the curriculum an established education practice or an unproven innovation? (b) What valid experimental research evidence (not testimonials) exists to demonstrate that the approach is effective? (c) Is an efficient, manageable accountability process built into the approach, including checkpoints to determine if the implementation is producing the intended benefits for students? (d) Is the approach equitable for children of poverty, students with disabilities, and students who do not speak English as their first language? (e) Are the costs of the approach and its implementation reasonable? (National Center to Improve the Tools of Educators, 1997a).

Teachers haven't been well trained. If something isn't working, it's hard to blame the teachers directly, but a commonly used reason for failure anywhere in the educational pipeline (especially from teachers themselves) is that they haven't received the kind of support and training they need to make a program successful. And this excuse works especially well when test scores in reading aren't up to par. Training teachers in the teaching of reading is complex, ongoing, and never ending. Find a way to provide the training your teachers need. Give it yourself if necessary.

Kids watch too much television. This excuse wins the prize for creativity. The blame for declining reading scores rests with inanimate objects that can't argue with us. There's a lot of research to support how many hours of a child's lifetime are spent in front of the "boob tube," and that makes a convincing case for its impact because students who are watching TV are clearly not reading at the same time.

Something to Think About: Find ways to get the students in your school to read recreationally. One of our most successful programs to increase the amount of time students spent reading was the Battle of the Books. See Chapter 6 for a more complete description of this program.

Our school entrance is a revolving door. This was an excuse I could always use when the achievement test scores didn't improve; close to 30% of our student population turned over each year. And it presented a very real instructional problem for the faculty. I could always count on several move-ins and move-outs the week before tests were administered. Naturally, the move-outs were top-notch students who had been with us since kindergarten. We'd nurtured them and taught them everything they knew. They were consistently above grade level. Naturally, the move-ins were all below-grade-level students who had spent their educational careers in a dozen different schools with no hope of any instructional continuity. Did they take the tests? Of course. They were our students. Were we happy about it? Never.

Something to Think About: We implemented a variety of measures to bring these students up to our expectations as quickly as we could. We called them Target Students, and teachers had a list of instructional strategies they used regularly with these students. Whenever direct instruction was completed and students were working independently, the teacher would automatically move to the desk or table of the Target Student to make sure he or she understood what was required. Target Students, especially those who had been enrolled in a large number of different schools, often had major gaps in their skills and needed constant monitoring and supervision to make sure they stayed tuned in and on task.

Our students are poor and disadvantaged. This explanation for low reading achievement feeds into the "low expectations" mentality. "What can you expect? Look where they come from."

Something to Think About: Automatically assuming that students who receive free and reduced lunch will score in the bottom quartile is a self-fulfilling prophecy. Read about the many schools in our country whose test results fly in the face of this fallacious assumption (Siegel, 1997).

On the Outside Looking In: What the Critics Charge Is Wrong With Reading Instruction

The critics of public education (parents, community activists, policy analysts, media, and politicians) have their own opinions about why our children aren't reading the way we want them to.

Ineffective instructional methods are being used. For some educational critics, the current learner-centered classroom lies at the heart of all of education's woes. In looking for the reasons why reading achievement has declined across our country, they find the culprit to be the demise of the "old-fashioned" classroom. They point to practices like the elimination of letter and number grades, the jettisoning of standardized testing and assessment, the elimination of textbooks and workbooks, and the emphasis on student-driven lessons and discussions (Brooks & Brooks, 1993) to be reason "numero uno" for the illiteracy problem. They believe that the role of the teacher should be first and foremost to teach. "This approach includes direct instruction, immediately responsive constructive criticism, coaching, and active monitoring of student work" (M. Damer, personal communication, November 3, 1997).

Students are using reading materials that have been dumbed down. Critics of education point to the fact that if students are always permitted to choose their own reading materials and never required to "stretch" themselves to read classics or more difficult selections, they will never develop the reading expertise needed for reading long passages of both fiction and nonfiction with comprehension. Parents are often dismayed to find that although their child is getting "good" grades in reading throughout the school year, the scores on a standardized test reflect below-grade-level achievement. In some school districts, teachers are not permitted to test student reading levels, making the matching of challenging reading material to students' levels impossible (M. Damer, personal communication, November 3, 1997).

Teachers and administrators have low expectations for students. The relationship between teacher expectations and student achievement is well documented (Treddlie, Kirby, & Stringfield, 1989). When student achievement is low, one must always look at the attitudes of teachers and administrators about those students. Teachers and administrators in effective schools treat students as if they are able. They ask challenging questions, expect work to be completed, and believe that all their students can learn. When teachers frequently complain about students, have poorly managed classrooms, and blame others for what is happening in their classroom, low expectations are rampant. The mere presence of the principal in his or her school's classrooms also has a powerful effect on student achievement (Andrews & Soder, 1987).

Schools are wasting too much time on nonacademics. Schools do spend a lot time on what I term the "touchy-feely" stuff. The critics are right. Even teachers complain about all of the interruptions. When schools are overloaded with assemblies, fund-raisers, intercom interruptions, field trips, birthday and holiday parties, pep assemblies, and the like, there is less time for instruction.

The reading curriculum is confused and watered down, and it doesn't get students off to a good start. Translated that means: "We're not teaching phonics first in the schools." There's a growing group of parents, politicians, and researchers who blame declining reading achievement on the fact that we're not teaching phonics. Reid Lyon, a neuropsychologist in charge of research for the National Institute of Child Health and Human Development, puts it this way: "People blame the kids, the teachers, the parents, the socioeconomic background, all kinds of things except the instructional procedures being used" (quoted in Lally & Price, 1997). It's not enough to integrate phonics with other instructional methodologies and introduce it incidentally. It must be taught first and as a self-contained unit of instruction to satisfy these folks. In fact, the conspicuous absence of any direct instruction using a phonic/linguistic program in the California state reading curriculum was directly blamed (among other factors) for the fact that California's fourth-grade children scored last in the national ranking of 39 participating states in reading, according to the 1994 NAEP. In 1995, the California Task Force on Reading concluded that mandating whole language statewide was a mistake. On September 12, 1995, the California legislature passed AB 170, which requires the state Board of Education to ensure that the materials it adopts for reading instruction include "systematic, explicit phonics." The vote was unanimous in both legislative chambers. The "phonics first folks" are convinced that reading scores in our country would soar if every school adopted a systematic phonics instruction program.

Schools are not teaching an adequate dose of skills and strategies. Decoding is just the beginning of learning to read. If a student cannot understand and remember the main idea that the words he or she is reading are conveying, reading is not really happening. Students must have a set of strategies to use much like a mechanic has a tool box, and without these strategies no wonder so many kids can't come up with the "right answers."

Teachers haven't had adequate preservice education. This is another good reason that is difficult to document and even more difficult to do anything about. If something isn't working, blame the colleges of education. Everyone knows those ivory tower types don't really care about what's happening in classrooms; they just need more research studies on their resumes. There is, however, a real concern about the one-sided "whole language" slant that nearly all beginning teachers are experiencing as well as worries about the scant number of class hours devoted to reading instruction.

> Elementary teachers report with alarming frequency that they have not been prepared to adequately teach reading; that many have only had, at most, two reading courses throughout their reading careers; that theory is never directly related to teaching practice with children and demonstrated explicitly by professors; that student teaching and practicum experiences are rarely thoughtfully integrated with college course work; that they have never observed a professor model and demonstrate teaching approaches with children of differing abilities in laboratory or classroom settings; and that their knowledge of individual differences in children is limited. (Lyon, 1997, p. 50)

Teachers are ineffective. The work of William Sanders has shown that the single biggest factor in the academic growth of students is the teacher (W. Sanders, personal communication, February 1997). The statistical model developed by Sanders and his colleagues, the Tennessee Value-Added Assessment System (TVAAS), albeit a controversial one, has yielded some startling findings that confirm what parents have always believed (Sanders & Rivers, 1996). When a child gets a bad teacher for 1 year, it hurts; when a child gets bad teachers for

14   THE PRINCIPAL'S GUIDE TO RAISING READING ACHIEVEMENT

2 years in a row, his or her educational progress can be in jeopardy. In Sanders and Rivers's (1996) study, fifth graders who had 3 years of teachers who were judged ineffective by their supervisors averaged 54 to 60 percentile points lower in achievement than did students who had teachers judged effective. And the results of the teacher effects (bad or good) carried forward and accumulated for as long as 2 years. Educational critics and parents point to just plain poor teaching as one of the reasons reading achievement is low.

The Experts Check In: Researchers, Consultants, Professors, and Other Ivory Tower Types

The final group to tell its "side of the story" is the experts, the folks who are supposed to know what they're doing so they can share their wisdom with the educators in the field. These are the people who should be "leading the way." Unfortunately for practitioners, there are two differing points of view regarding reading instruction. And even more unfortunately, these points of view have become politicized. In the minds of many, if you're for kids, you're for whole language, and you're a right-wing fundamentalist if you're for phonics. Although many educators strive to be balanced or eclectic in their approach to reading instruction, the advocates of both points of view are often religious in their fervor to demonstrate the sins of "the opposition." Chapter 2 contains a lengthy discussion of the "great debate" or "the reading wars" as they have come to be known as well as more complete definitions of phonics and whole language. Understanding this background will be important as you lead your faculty to consider how to bring a balanced, research-based approach to improving your school's reading achievement.

The Phonics Faction: "We're depriving students of the ability to decode words, a skill they need to have to be successful readers." This "camp" (and unfortunately, it sometimes seems as if a war really is going on) believes that if every school would include sequential, explicit, and direct phonics instruction beginning in kindergarten and continuing through first grade, reading achievement in this country would increase dramatically, especially for the nearly 40% of the population who have reading problems. Those who are fervent in their campaign to make phonics instruction mandatory for every student point to the findings from 30 years of research at the National Institute of Child Health and Human Development as all the proof that is needed for educators to change their ways (Grossen, 1996). They do not subscribe to the theory that all children will learn to read naturally, as they learn to talk. They believe that reading is not developmental but learned. Although the "phonics first" advocates agree with the whole-language purists that students should read outstanding literature and find meaning in everything they read, they do not advocate teaching sound-spelling relationships simply as an incidental part of reading real stories. They believe that phonics instruction must be taught first, separately, and sequentially.

The Whole-Language Gurus: We're teaching "drill and kill" and ruining our children's interest in and love for reading. Lining up on the opposite end of the reading instruction continuum are the whole-language proponents, who believe that phonics drills, workbook pages, and controlled-vocabulary readers using words that fit into common phonic patterns will destroy any child's love of reading. Ken Goodman (1993), whole-language guru, says that

> if children come to read and write through these programs, it's not because of the programs, but because of the ability of most children to learn language, including reading and writing, in spite of obstacles put in their way. Fortunately, no one has yet been able to devise an instructional program so bad that it has succeeded in keeping the majority of pupils from learning. (p. 107)

Of those children who are having difficulty in learning to read, Goodman (1993) says that

> too much out-of-context and uninformed phonics can produce problems for precisely those children who are less likely to succeed in our schools. They are made to believe that reading is word recognition, so they think that if they can't recognize words immediately, or sound them out, they can never become literate. They become their own worst enemies as they accept the blame for their lack of success. (p. 111)

Other whole-language proponents assert that many poorer readers have had an overdose of phonics with little regard for meaning (Carbo, 1987; Chomsky, 1976; Meek, 1983). In fact, says Smith (1985b),

> Phonics, which means teaching a set of spelling-to-sound correspondence rules that permit the "decoding" of written language into speech, just does not work. To expect any readers, and especially beginners, to learn and rely upon phonics is to distract them with involved and unreliable procedures that are in fact largely unnecessary. (p. 49)

What's a Principal to Do?

As you face the constant hammering of educational critics and the often confusing research and counterclaims by "experts," what can you do if you want to raise reading achievement in your school? Here's where to begin.

First, think for yourself. Read, learn, discuss, network, and begin to trust your own instincts. You and your staff must determine what is best for your school. It won't be easy. As Terrence Deal (1986) points out,

> Each approach has a cadre of gurus, scholars, advocates, and disciples who righteously defend one view against criticism from other camps. The end result is a cacophony of voices; a dialogue of the deaf among academics, usually a source of confusion among those struggling to improve schools. (p. 122)

Read all of the books and articles in Resource B: Recommended Reading List, at the end of this book. Become a thoughtful learner. Design your own site-based research in which you genuinely evaluate the results of a curriculum or program you are using. Take control of your school's destiny.

Second, begin to focus your attention and that of your faculty on what Benjamin Bloom (1980) called the "alterable variables," those things that you can change. Don't spend your time worrying about or blaming things over which you have no control (e.g., characteristics of your student and parent population). Rather, focus your energy and creativity on what you can change (e.g., the amount of time the school or individual teachers spend teaching a subject; the amount of time that students are actually on task in the classroom; the types of materials and instructional strategies teachers are using; the effectiveness of the teachers on your staff). You can't change the intelligence of the students who are enrolled in your school, but you can teach them the prerequisite skills they need to be successful in a learning task. You can't change the socioeconomic status or educational level of their parents, but you can develop collaborative programs to work with and inform parents about subjects like discipline, reading aloud, and the importance of homework. You have only so many hours in the school day, but you can figure out ways to make better use of that time. You can't always change the teachers on your staff, but you can help them to increase their effectiveness.

Finally, become an instructional leader. This is much easier said than done. The need for more skills and training and the lack of support from superintendents, school boards, and community, plus our own personal lack of vision, will, or courage, can stand in the way. But you have no choice. The most powerful research to date on the impact of strong instructional leadership on student achievement comes from Andrews and Soder (1987). Their findings showed that the normal equivalent gain scores of students in schools led by strong instructional leaders, as perceived by the teachers in their respective schools, were significantly greater in both total reading and total mathematics than those of students in schools rated as having average or weak leaders.

The chapters ahead will provide you with the information, research, ideas, inspiration, and motivation you need to lead your school to excellence in reading achievement.

2

The Great Debate

Phonics Versus Whole Language

One of the most heartbreaking sights in American schools today is that of children—once so eager to read—discovering that they are not learning how. There comes over those sparkling eyes a glaze of listless despair. We are not talking about a few children and scattered schools. We are talking about millions of children and every school in the nation. And the toll in young spirits is the least of it. The toll in the learning and thinking potential of our citizenry is beyond measure.

Sylvia Farnham-Diggory
(quoted in Spalding & Spalding, 1957/1990, p. 10)

When my first child went off to kindergarten, I experienced all the usual emotions. Not only was she leaving the nest, but in those new surroundings she would be instructed, examined, and evaluated. Would she measure up? Would she have fun? Would she like school? And most important to me, would she learn to read? I already knew my daughter liked books. I read aloud to her daily. I also knew that she understood and remembered a great deal of what we read together. But I had no idea if she could or even would learn to read with ease. My earlier attempts at teaching her had not been notable. I had purchased a "miracle" toilet training book that promised success in less than a day. Consequently, I didn't even attempt to teach her to read. I decided the joyful experience we shared together with books was too special to turn it into a battleground.

She went off to kindergarten with anticipation and was not disappointed. One day in early October, she arrived home and announced, "I learned to read today." I couldn't believe what I was hearing. Perhaps she had confused writing letters on paper with reading. "Can you read for me?" I asked her with barely contained excitement. To this point she had never read a single word aloud to me.

Eagerly, I pulled out a library book she had never seen before. She promptly began reading aloud to me with fluency and expression as if this were something we had been doing regularly.

In actuality, reading aloud was something we had been doing regularly. Only now the roles were reversed. My child was reading to me. And I realized that in her mind, she *had* learned to read in 1 day at school. She was not yet aware that the preparation for this moment when she was actually reading had been going on since she was an infant. The preparation for this moment had been 5 years of continuing conversation, incessant questions, endless repetitions of nursery rhymes and poems, and the reading aloud of hundreds of her favorite picture books—a "whole language" approach to be sure. I began implementing it in utero. I believe reading aloud is the single most important thing that parents can do to ensure school success for their children. But is it the way most children learn to read? Absolutely not, as my second child's experience will indicate.

I fully expected my daughter's story to repeat itself when I sent my son off to kindergarten 2 years later. After all, he was going to the same school, had the same teacher, and had experienced 5 years of the same reading-rich environment. There was absolutely no reason to think that his experiences with reading would be any different than his sister's. He wasn't an at-risk child. He was a bright and eager learner. October came and went, however, and he didn't come home to tell me he had learned to read. He learned his sounds and began to blend simple words but he never read aloud to me with fluency as his sister had done. Under the wise guidance of his teacher, I never prodded or pushed. In first grade, he completed a phonics program along with a basal reading series. We continued to read aloud every night. He read to me from simple readers, slowly and haltingly at first. He sounded out each word carefully, but experienced success every step of the way.

In second grade, all of the pieces of the puzzle fell into place for him and he truly began to read, over 1,000 books actually. By spring, he was reading full-length novels by E. B. White and Beverly Cleary. How did he get to that point? Teachers who recognized his academic needs and met them and a curriculum that skillfully integrated a variety of learning materials and approaches but was built on a strong phonics foundation. What could account for the difference in how my children learned to read? Their sex? Perhaps. Their developmental readiness? Maybe. Differences in learning style? An idea worth considering. But who cares now? They are both successful university graduates. Might the scenario have been different if my son had not experienced "phonics first"? Might my daughter's delight in reading everything she could get her hands on have been destroyed if teachers had not recognized her reading precocity and nurtured it? I don't even want to think about it.

What is the point of this personal story? Simply this: As educators, we are doing a terrible disservice to our students by failing to recognize the importance of using a balanced approach to beginning reading instruction. If how we teach our children to read becomes a political football rather than an educational issue, we all stand to lose.

The "reading wars," or "the great debate" as the controversy between whole-language and phonics proponents has come to be known, provide a fascinating, if confusing, backdrop against which to examine beginning reading instruction. How did something so elemental to the entire schooling process, how students learn to read, become so controversial? And how can you as a practitioner make sense of the claims and counterclaims and do what is best for your students? Even after you've taught your students to read, don't expect to be "home free." The debate rages on. Exactly what should they be reading? Is there a body of knowledge, as suggested by E. D. Hirsch (1987), that the educated and literate individual should be expected to know? And if so, what is our responsibility as educators to impart that knowledge? In the chapter ahead we'll meet the key players in this controversy, get a crash course on terminology, discover that the critical issues are much larger than "Which series shall we pick?" and frame the questions you will need to answer for yourself before you can lead your school to instructional excellence and increased reading achievement.

The Reading Instruction Glossary: Key Words to Know

Before you tackle a brief history of the reading wars, you'll need some vocabulary review and possibly even a spelling lesson. Although you won't have to write each word 10 times and there won't be a quiz on Friday, a knowledge of this terminology will certainly increase your comprehension score on the standardized test in May.

1. *Cognitive strategies:* heuristics (i.e., methods that when taught to students will enable them to find solutions and answers for themselves). Rosenshine defines them as "procedures that students can use to help them understand and address higher-order tasks in areas such as reading comprehension and writing" (quoted in Pressley, Woloshyn, & Associates, 1995, p. iii).

2. *Developmental:* natural, something that will happen gradually over time as a child matures and cannot be taught; in the reading literature, the opposite of "learned."

3. *Decoding:* the ability to look at the printed page and translate it into language; an important prerequisite to the ability to decode is phonemic awareness (Stanovich, 1993).

4. *Direct instruction:* when the term appears in lower case (direct instruction), it refers to a style of teaching in which the teacher is "in charge" and has carefully structured the presentation as well as the responses desired from students. When the term appears capitalized (Direct Instruction), it refers to a specific teaching style originally developed at the University of Oregon (see Resource C at the end of this book for the Web site).

5. *Fluency:* automaticity and flow in the act of reading. The act of repetitive decoding of a particular word helps to establish the spelling patterns of that word in memory. The most effective way for students to become fluent with a specific word is for them to consciously process both the letter patterns and sounds of the word the first few times it is read (Share, 1995; Share & Stanovich, 1995).

6. *"Matthew effect":* has its origins in the New Testament parable of the talents in which "the rich get richer and the poor get poorer": "For to every one who has will more be given, and he will have abundance; but from him who has not, even what he has will be taken away from him" (Matthew 25:29, Revised Standard Version). The term is used to describe the effect of reading deficits in phonemic awareness in kindergarten and first grade from which "poor" students almost never recover (Stanovich, 1986).

7. *Phoneme:* the most basic element of the language system; a sound. Phonemes are very important on the reading scene today, and much of the new research revolves around them (Grossen, 1996).

8. *Phonemic awareness:* the ability to recognize individual sounds in words (e.g., rhyming, blending spoken sounds into words, counting phonemes); a critical prerequisite to being able to learn to read. Lack of phonemic awareness in kindergarten or first grade is the single best predictor of a future reading problem (Grossen, 1996). Also known as phonological awareness. Whole-language proponents definitely qualify this definition: "ability to detect sounds in speech that *are supposed to be* [italics added] represented by the letters of the alphabet (Smith, 1994, p. 312).

9. *Phonics:* a term that has become a code word or rallying cry for those who support teaching basic skills in a direct and sequential way. Parents even label schools as "phonics schools" or "whole-language schools" even though phonics instruction at its very best will consume no more than half of the language arts activities in kindergarten and/or first grade. Phonics (stripped of its political baggage) is an instructional method for teaching students to sound out words rather than reading them as a "whole" or "guessing" what they might be on the basis of context. Smith (1994) defines phonics as "reading instruction based on the *assumption* [italics added] that reading is decoding to sound and requires learning spelling-to-sound correspondences" (p. 312).

10. *Psycholinguistics:* an area of common concern in psychology and linguistics studying how individuals learn and use language (Smith, 1994, p. 312).

11. *Reading:* a process in which information from the text and the knowledge possessed by the reader act together to produce meaning (National Academy of Education, Commission on Reading, 1985, p. 8).

12. *Sight words:* words that students have memorized and can read on sight.

13. *Whole language:* Ken Goodman describes it this way: "a pedagogy, or a way that teachers think about teaching; a bringing together [of] everything we've learned about how language works in terms of learning [and] how learning to read and write is an extension of oral language" (quoted in Martinez, 1997, p. 11). Frank Smith (1994) defines whole language as "an educational movement based on the belief that language learning takes place most effectively when learners are engaged collaboratively in meaningful and purposeful uses of language, as opposed to exercises, drills, and tests. Sometimes referred to as the naturalistic approach or (misleadingly) as child-centered learning, and known

in Britain as real books. Frequently contrasted with direct instruction" (p. 313). Some critics charge that whole language is only the most recent incarnation of other methods such as "look and say," "sight method," and "whole word."

The Reading Wars: A Crash Course in History

It's an ugly battle between the whole-language proponents and the phonics folks, one that has been raging on and off for a couple of hundred years. Oh, the terminology that is used, the protagonists in the debate, and the sophistication of the research have all changed, but the basic conflict still boils down to the question of how children best learn to read. You've already been introduced to the two principal schools of thought in Chapter 1. Here's a brief timeline of how this conflict has evolved over decades and where we are today.

Whole Language Versus Phonics Timeline

• 1500-146 B.C.: The Phoenicians invent the alphabet and reading is taught by memorizing the sounds of syllables and blending them together to make words (Mitchell, 1977).

• 1783: Noah Webster publishes his *Blue-Backed Speller* and has this to say about the competition: "Among the defects and absurdities found in books of this kind hitherto published, we may rank the want of a thorough investigation of the sounds in the English language, and the powers of the several letters—the promiscuous arrangement of words in the same table. In attempting to correct these faults it was necessary to begin with the elements of the language and explain the powers of the letters" (quoted in Flesch, 1955, p. 45).

• 1791: German educator Professor Friedrich Gedike, director of the Kölnische Gymnasium in Berlin, publishes the first look-and-say primer (Mathews, 1966, p. 15).

• 1837: Horace Mann, educational reformer and secretary of the Massachusetts Board of Education, denounces the letters of the alphabet as "bloodless, ghostly apparitions that were responsible for steeping children's faculties in lethargy" (quoted in Levine, 1994, p. 40).

• 1908: Edmund Burke Huey (1908) writes in *The Psychology and Pedagogy of Reading* that "the technique of reading should not appear in the early years, and the very little early work that should be tolerated in phonics should be entirely distinct from reading" (p. 21).

• 1929: Arthur I. Gates of Columbia University and William S. Gray of the University of Chicago each produce look-and-say readers, Gates for Scott, Foresman and Gray for Macmillan (Flesch, 1981, p. 23).

• 1930s-1950s: The consensus in beginning reading instruction as reflected in textbooks for teachers and published series for students emphasizes recognition of sight words (Chall, 1967/1983, pp. 14-15). Drill and practice in phonics in isolation is not recommended: "The child should not isolate sounds and blend them to form words. Instead he should identify unknown words through a process of visual analysis and substitution" (Gray, 1948/1960, p. 15).

- 1937: Samuel Orton publishes his pioneering study *Reading, Writing, and Speech Problems in Children* and suggests that the look-and-say method may have some problems. "I think we can show [that] this technique [sight reading or look and say] is not only not adapted but often proves an actual obstacle to reading progress" (Orton, 1937/1989, p. 199).

- 1955: *Why Johnny Can't Read* by Rudolph Flesch explodes onto the best-seller list. Flesch (1955) blames the "word method" for just about everything that's wrong with the country and politicized what had heretofore been a largely educational issue: "I say, therefore, that the word method [look-say/whole language] is gradually destroying democracy in this country; it returns to the upper middle class the privileges that public education was supposed to distribute evenly among the people. The American Dream is, essentially, equal opportunity through free education for all. This dream is beginning to vanish in a country where the public schools are falling down on the job" (p. 132).

- 1957: In *The Writing Road to Reading*, Romalda Spalding presents a comprehensive method for teaching children to read using phonics: "It is safe to say that most school officials now assert that their schools teach all methods [both phonics and whole word]. Unfortunately however, very, very few teachers today know enough about phonics to teach it accurately. Very few teachers' colleges in the country give a separate, full course in phonics. One reading of this book will make clear that a teacher does need to study and learn phonics thoroughly before teaching it" (Spalding & Spalding, 1957/1990, p. 18).

- 1965: Louise Gurren and Ann Hughes (1965) conclude after reviewing 36 studies that "rigorous controlled research clearly favors the teaching of all of the main sound-symbol relationships, both vowel and consonant, from the start of formal reading instruction" (p. 344).

- 1967: *Learning to Read: The Great Debate* tries to strike a chord for balance and ecumenicism, but with author Jeanne Chall's (1967/1983) recommendation that "a code emphasis tends to produce better overall reading achievement by the beginning of fourth grade than a meaning emphasis" (p. 137), she positioned herself squarely in the camp of the phonics folks.

- 1975: The basal reading series used in American classrooms become more eclectic including systematic instruction in spelling-to-sound correspondences along with stories and exercises to develop and reinforce comprehension skills (Popp, 1975).

- 1977: The results of Project Follow-Through, the world's largest educational experiment begun as part of Lyndon Johnson's War on Poverty, are published (Stebbins, St. Pierre, & Proper, 1977). Out of three major models selected for evaluation, only the Direct Instruction model emphasizing the teaching of phonemic awareness and phonics brings children close to the 50th percentile in all subject areas.

• 1980: A pair of reading researchers presenting at the annual conference of the Orton Society choose their side in the battle: "If war should break out between those, in Chall's terms, who emphasize the code and those who emphasize meaning in reading instruction we would enlist under the banner of the code. But let no one say we claim that decoding is all there is to reading. Our view of reading, that it consists of decoding plus linguistic comprehension, may be too simple. If so, it should be easy to refute, for it holds that any child with normal comprehension who learns to decode with facility will know how to read, and if any child with normal comprehension fails to read, it is because he has not learned to decode with facility" (Gough & Hillinger, 1980, pp. 193-194).

• 1981: The National Institute of Education decides not to disseminate the successful results of the Direct Instruction model in Project Follow-Through because "the audience for evaluations is an audience of teachers to whom appeals to the need for accountability for public funds or the rationality of science are largely irrelevant" (Glass & Camilli, 1981, p. 31).

• 1983: Chall updates her 1967 edition of *Learning to Read: The Great Debate*, but does not reverse her position on phonics.

• 1985: Frank Smith (1985b), psycholinguist and apologist for whole language, weighs in with his opinion on how children learn to read: "Children cannot be taught to read. A teacher's responsibility is not to teach children to read but to make it possible for them to learn to read" (p. 7).

• 1985: *Becoming a Nation of Readers: The Report of the Commission on Reading* is released by the National Institute of Education. Although the report recommends that children spend less time completing workbooks and skill sheets and more time in independent reading (National Academy of Education, Commission on Reading, 1985, p. 119), it also includes this recommendation relative to phonics instruction: "The issue is no longer, as it was several decades ago, whether children should be taught phonics. The issues now are specific ones of just how it should be done" (p. 36).

• 1986: Ken Goodman (1986), whole-language guru, explains how phonics instruction actually makes things worse rather than better: "Many school traditions seem to have actually hindered language development. In our zeal to make it easy, we've made it hard. How? Primarily by breaking whole (natural) language up into bite-size, but abstract little pieces. It seemed so logical to think that little children could best learn simple little things. We took apart the language and turned it into words, syllables, and isolated sounds. Unfortunately, we also postponed its natural purpose—the communication of meaning—and turned it into a set of abstractions, unrelated to the needs and experiences of the children we sought to help" (p. 7).

- 1987: A survey of 43 texts used to train teachers of reading finds that none advocates systematic phonics instruction and only 9 even mention that there was a debate on the issue (Levine, 1994, p. 41).

- 1988: California mandates the exclusive use of literature-based instruction (whole language) for teaching beginning reading (Diegmueller, 1995).

- 1988: Marie Carbo, advocate of reading instruction designed to mesh with children's learning styles, takes on Jeanne Chall and phonics in *Phi Delta Kappan.* Although Carbo (1988) purports to neither support nor oppose either point of view (phonics or whole language), she takes her gloves off on the first page: "If phonics is so effective and so much of it has been taught for the past 20 years, one might reasonably ask why the U.S. ranks 49th in literacy" (p. 226).

- 1989: Jeanne Chall (1989) has her day in court and responds to Carbo: "I recommended [in *Learning to Read: The Great Debate* (1967/1983, pp. 307-313)] a code emphasis only as a beginning reading method—a method to start the child on, and I did not recommend ignoring reading for meaning practice. I recommended changes to be made in basal readers to improve their content, including more literature and harder reading matter. I also recommended that library books, rather than workbooks, be used by children not working with the teacher and that writing be incorporated into the teaching of reading" (p. 525).

- 1989: The beat goes on and Marie Carbo (1989) fires yet another salvo: "Chall's pro-phonics position may stem from her theories, not from the research she reviewed" (p. 155).

- 1990: In a comprehensive review of the reading instruction literature, Marilyn Jager Adams (1990) concludes that "before children will learn to read, they must learn to recognize individual letters. They must become aware of the structure of language, from sentences and words to phonemes. And, most important, they must develop a basic understanding of the forms and functions of text and of its personal value to their own lives" (p. 422).

- 1994: Marie Carbo is still debunking the great phonics myth: "The need for any explicit phonics instruction is a myth" (quoted in Levine, 1994, p. 41).

- 1994: Frank Smith (1994), in the fifth edition of his reading text *Understanding Reading: A Psycholinguistic Analysis of Reading and Learning to Read,* asserts that "the difficulty many children experience in learning phonics rules, or indeed in making sense of them, has led to the notion that such children lack 'phonological awareness,' that is, the ability to deconstruct the sounds of spoken words. It is taken for granted that the tenuous relationship between letters and sounds must be of central importance to readers of alphabetic writing systems (compared with readers of nonalphabetic systems like Chinese)—why else have an alphabet? The alternative point of view, which may be slowly gaining ground, is that the alphabet primarily serves writing and should make no substantial difference to reading" (p. 148).

- 1995: Reid Lyon, director of research for the National Institute of Child Health and Human Development (NICHHD), testifies before a U.S. Senate subcommittee that "most reading disabilities stem from a deficit in the most basic level of the language system—the phoneme" (quoted in Diegmueller, 1996, p. 33).

- 1995: The American Federation of Teachers (AFT) casts its vote in favor of phonics first. In opening remarks to an entire issue of their publication *American Educator* devoted to reading instruction, the editor, Elizabeth McPike (1995), has this to say: "The Whole Language movement has brought to the forefront many complex and legitimate issues about the nature of teaching and learning and the goals of education, and it has brought fresh life to many classrooms. But to the extent that it has reduced decoding to an incidental place in the reading curriculum, it has done a terrible disservice to the children whose lives depend on mastery of that skill" (p. 6).

- 1995: California passes the ABC law (AB 170) requiring state officials to make sure that adopted materials give adequate attention to systematic explicit phonics, spelling, and computational skills (Manzo, 1997a).

- 1996: Marie Carbo (1996) starts to waffle a bit. In an article titled "Whole Language or Phonics? Use Both," she concedes that some kids may not learn to read efficiently when a whole-language approach is used: "Whole language can feel disorganized and haphazard to analytic learners. If the modeling of stories is too infrequent or if the teacher does not provide enough interesting repetition, such youngsters can fall behind quickly. Since the systematic teaching of phonics is not emphasized [in whole-language instruction] some children may not develop the tools they need for decoding words" (p. 61).

- 1996: Ken Goodman insists that the flap over the method (whole language) is really an effort by cultural conservatives to discredit public education—and thus win support for tax-supported vouchers for private schools (Duff, 1996, p. A-9).

- 1996: Bill Honig (1996), former California state superintendent of instruction, reverses his earlier stand in support of whole language and writes a book (*Teaching Our Children to Read: The Role of Skills in a Comprehensive Reading Program*, Corwin Press) exposing "whole language myths." "The erroneous belief that almost all students can learn to read without an organized, explicit skill strand has taken root in too many schools and districts with disastrous results" (p. 5).

- 1996: Regie Routman (1996), a teacher pioneer in whole-language instruction, suggests what's gone wrong with whole language: "Those of us from a skills-oriented background kept what we knew worked. We could pick and choose. But other colleagues (some recent graduates and some veteran teachers too) never learned how to teach the cueing systems or integrated skills into the curriculum. They didn't understand what teaching skills in context meant" (p. 36). Susan Church (1996) concurs: "This issue of 'children falling through the cracks' or what some call 'the hole in whole language' is pervasive." She goes on to say later in her remarks that her concern "is not that whole language theory is lacking, but that many children are not learning to read and write because of the way that theory has been enacted in practice" (p. 34).

• 1997: The NICHHD releases a study by Barbara Foorman concluding that "direct phonics instruction should be the first in a sequence of methods used to teach some students to read" (quoted in Manzo, 1997b, p. 1). The news appears on the front page of *Education Week*.

• 1997: The debate begins anew as Gerald S. Coles (1997), whole-language apologist, has this to say about the study in a letter to the editor of *Education Week:* "Considering its serious scientific limitations, the study certainly rates neither front-page coverage nor credibility in policy decisions on literacy education" (p. 45).

• 1997: Reid Lyon (1997), director of research at NICHHD, responds to Coles's assertion: "In fact, research conducted under the auspices of the National Institutes of Health in general, and the National Institute of Child Health and Human Development in this particular case, must meet the highest levels of scientific integrity, review and application. . . . In addition, the NICHHD reading-intervention studies must investigate reading development and disorders within a longitudinal perspective that begins with children before they enter the 1st grade and follows them for at least five years" (p. 50).

• 1997: California's state school board adopts a list of materials approved for purchase in the state that contain basic reading skills and an emphasis on phonics. Materials published by Rigby and the Wright Group (publishers of books and materials widely used in whole-language classrooms) are not included on the approved list (Manzo, 1997a).

• 1997: Ken Goodman calls the adoption an "example of the hysteria that is affecting decision making in education" (quoted in Manzo, 1997a).

• 1997: In a *Time* magazine cover story, the author concluded: "After reviewing the arguments mustered by the phonics and whole-language proponents, can we make a judgment as to who is right? Yes. The value of explicit, systematic phonics instruction has been well established" (Collins, 1997, p. 81).

Why Are We Divided?

Although more and more of the reading literature is beginning to include terms like *balanced, eclectic, integrated,* and *contextual* when referring to the relationship of phonics and whole language in reading instruction, certainty regarding just what they should be doing in their schools seems to elude a vast number of educators. Our schoolchildren are paying the price for this confusion with poor reading achievement. Based on my personal experiences as a parent and educator and after an extensive review of the literature, I must agree with Reid Lyon, who states: "There is no debate. At a certain stage of reading, phonics is necessary. Then children need literature to read. Why we polarize it is a mystery to me" (quoted in Lally & Price, 1997). I have three answers to Dr. Lyon's question: politics, professors, and profits.

Politics. When "phonics" became a rallying cry for political entities and special-interest groups as opposed to an instructional methodology, common sense on both ends of the political (and educational) continuum disappeared. For example, the Freedom Party of Ontario, Canada has adopted a rabid stance on phonics claiming that it is "a complete method of teaching reading." They assert with a naïveté that is amusing that "these other skills [inferencing, drawing conclusions, locating meaning] are not something we include in our definition of reading" (Freedom Party of Ontario, 1997).

Educators, however, are just as guilty of overgeneralizing. Mary Damer (personal communication, July 13, 1997), founder of the Taxpayers for Academic Priorities in St. Charles Schools (TAPIS), has been involved since college in liberal politics; she met her husband, a history professor, at a peace march. Damer chuckles as she relates the district's response to the questions she and a group initially raised about curricula. "They sent out packets to all of the teachers explaining how to deal with right-wing tactics. We just wanted to know whether there was any research to support the decisions they were making."

The discussion has become so politicized at some levels that Harvey Daniels (1996), an Illinois consultant and whole-language apologist, has given this advice to teachers: "It seems easier to drop the terminology—to simply be a holistic teacher, rather than talk about it. Why not quietly attend the meeting of your local TAWL [the Association of Whole Language] (soon to be picketed just like abortion clinics, no doubt), and rename your classroom program 'integrated.' "

Professors. Academic types are a second stumbling block to a meaningful dialogue between whole-language and phonics proponents. When an academic has staked an entire career on a philosophical point of view, done reams of research, and written widely, that individual (and his or her disciples) will not give up without a "fight." E. D. Hirsch (1996) describes this state of affairs as an "intellectual monopoly" and suggests that university professors, especially those in departments of teacher education, exert an enormous influence that does not always serve the best interests of students. "Despite the myth of local control, the intellectual monopoly ruling American K-12 education is more pervasive and harmful than the merely bureaucratic control exercised in other liberal democracies. Its prevailing ideas are more extreme and process-dominated than those found in systems that are more successful than our own" (Hirsch, 1996, p. 66).

Profits. The third and final obstacle in the way of discourse without rancor has to do with money. Textbook companies, trade book companies, and thousands of consultants are constantly trying to figure out which way the winds of research are blowing and then to develop reading programs and staff development seminars to meet the needs of districts. This is a billion dollar business, and turning the ship around in midcourse is very costly.

Where Do You Stand?

Do you know what you believe about beginning reading instruction? Patrick Groff (1991), a professor at San Diego State University, surveyed first- and second-grade teachers in San Diego, California. He found that for the most part teachers believed one thing and were doing (or claimed to be doing) something different). Take this short agree/disagree quiz yourself to see what you believe about how reading should be taught.

1. Children learn to read best the same way they learned to speak.
2. Children can teach themselves to read. Formal instruction is unnecessary.
3. Children should not learn reading subskills in any type of instructional sequence or "hierarchical" order.
4. Children should guess at written words, using sentence context cues.
5. Children should be taught to recognize words by sight as wholes.
6. The length and complexity of words is of little consequence in beginning reading instruction.
7. The intensive systematic teaching of phonics hinders reading comprehension.
8. Intensive phonics makes it more difficult for children to recognize words.
9. No workbooks or worksheets should ever be used.
10. English is spelled too unpredictably for phonics to work.

Directions for scoring the survey and the sources for the quotations on which these statements were based can be found in Resource A at the end of this book.

How Can You Make Sense of This Debate?

The best way to make sense of the debate for yourself is to do your homework. As you've often, I'm sure, told the students in your school: "No pain, no gain." A list of the books I suggest you read to gain a perspective on the "great debate" can be found in Resource B. If you don't make up your own mind about what you believe and how you want to lead your school, someone else will do it for you (e.g., staff, textbook publisher, district office, or state board).

Consulting books is just one way you can locate information regarding reading instruction. You can also let your fingers do the walking and have immediate access to a variety of interesting Web sites (and their links) via your computer and modem. I've included some of the more interesting ones in Resource C. Please accept my apologies in advance for any changes that may have occurred; technology is marvelous but not always as reliable and permanent as the printed page.

Who Can You Believe?

I have come to believe that defining good reading instruction is very similar to the proverbial blind men describing an elephant. Each of the men talked about the animal very differently depending on their vantage point. And the same thing is true when one examines reading instruction. It all depends on your perspective. Are you standing in the opening weeks of first grade? Or are you talking about 10-year-olds? Are you observing the reading landscape from your school media center? Or are you in the middle of a remedial class? In my opinion, one simple, all-purpose answer to the question of effective reading instruction does not exist. Some are trying to create this answer by using buzzwords like *eclectic, balanced, integrated,* and *contextual.* Grand words, to be sure, but how do they relate to Monday morning? More important than asserting that instruction in your school is balanced and integrated is to determine (together with your faculty) specific answers to the following questions. Consider bringing parents into this discussion as well.

• How should we teach beginning reading? Laying a secure foundation is critical because if students cannot read they will not only fail reading but also every other subject. The "Matthew effect" will kick in and ensure substandard performance by your students as they progress through your school. Deciding what beginning reading instruction in your school will look like is the first step.

• What kind of instruction do students need once they have learned to read? What kinds of materials should they be reading? How much time should they spend in reading instruction and in recreational reading? How will their parents be expected to contribute to the reading program? How important are skills and strategies in reading instruction? Which ones should be taught and when?

• Are philosophy, instruction, and curricula cohesive and articulated through all of the grades and by all of the teachers in the school? Students (and parents) are frequently confused and frustrated by the lack of organization in reading instruction (e.g., students read the same titles in several different grade levels; expectations are different depending on teachers at a given grade level; the teachers teach what they want to instead of according to an agreed-on plan). Everyone needs to be on the same page (not literally, but instructionally and philosophically). Reading instruction cannot be left to chance.

• What kinds of students make up my school population? Do I have a majority of at-risk students, or do my students arrive at school with all of the prerequisites firmly in place? What does my parent population expect from our schools with regard to teaching the children? Your choice of materials, techniques, and programs will be affected by the demographics of your students.

• Who are my teachers? Are they experienced veterans or recent graduates? Are they innovators eager to try everything new, or more conservative, show-me types? Do they have the knowledge, experience, and cognitive abilities to be prescriptive and eclectic, or are they poorly trained (preservice or postservice), confused (too many innovations too fast without support), and unfocused (fuzzy or poorly defined learning outcomes and lack of definitive curricula)?

I'm not expecting you'll do all of this homework without a tutor. Chapter 3 will describe how to work with your faculty to find these answers, and Chapter 4 will provide research-based essential learnings for students in Grades K-8.

What's a Principal to Do?

At this point, it's time to be reminded again of the main idea of this book: We can, whenever and wherever we choose, successfully teach all children to read. We already have reams of research, hundreds of successful programs, and thousands of effective schools to show us the way. Whether or not we do it must finally depend on how we feel about the fact that we haven't so far.

How do you feel about the fact that your school is not where you want it to be? Defensive, energized, inquisitive, motivated, paralyzed, angry, confused, exhausted, cynical, curious, or goal directed? All of these feelings are valid considering the daily demands that are made on you as a building leader. But as my sainted father used to say: "Enough of this standing around and talking. Get to work."

Your mission, raising reading achievement in your school—should you choose to accept it—is outlined in Chapter 3. You will need at least 5 years to complete your mission, so don't plan on going anywhere for a while. And here is what you must do:

1. Refine and perfect your own instructional leadership skills.

2. Structure a shared decision-making system in your school.

3. Develop sound, research-based learning objectives and select a curriculum and learning materials to meet these objectives.

4. Expect hard work, commitment to mission, and excellence from both your teachers and students.

What Do You Need to Make It Happen?

Principals who serve as the instructional leaders in their schools must ensure that their teachers are using the most effective methods and materials for teaching *all* students to read. The notion that children who are poor or disadvantaged, who come to school "less ready" than their peers, or who have uninvolved parents cannot learn to read is wrong!

Ian Hasbrouck
(personal communication,
December 12, 1997)

We are all on the lookout for the "magic bullet" or the "quick fix," a program we can implement and have instant results. Whether it be staff development or a teacher-proof curriculum, educators are easy marks for what Venezky calls "snake oil and charismatic solutions" (quoted in Palmaffy, 1997). We are easily bored by regularity and consistency and are constantly about the change process. Our quest for important and meaningful change, however, is an elusive one.

> For more than a hundred years much complaint has been made of the unmethodological way in which schools are conducted, but it is only within the last thirty that any serious attempt has been made to find a remedy for this state of things. And with what results? Schools remain exactly as they were. (Comenius, 1632/1967, p. 295)

Often the innovation we adopt is merely "snake oil" and we're delighted when it dies a natural death; we surreptitiously stash the manuals, thousands of dollars worth of expensive equipment, and dusty binders filled with consultants' handouts into the dumpster and thankfully move on to the next "implementation." But sometimes worthy, research-based improvements that should become institu-tionalized because they get results simply fail for the following reasons:

- Doing something brand new takes more work, and not everyone em-braces working harder. Consultants are good at making complicated things seem simple during their "dog and pony shows," but when the consultants fly home, the practitioners are left to "make it happen."

- Educators forget (if they ever really understood) that the innovations they adopted to "change the kids" usually require that they change also. Principals and teachers may be required to give up long-standing past practices and learn different methodologies. Most educators don't rank high on the risk-taking scale and if the leap of faith is too large, they will remain quietly on the sidelines of disbelief.

- Change requires discipline. Learning to do something new requires atten-tion to detail, practice of unfamiliar skills, and the desire for further training. These processes demand collaboration and teamwork, whereas typical teachers enjoy autonomy, routine, and the freedom to "do their own thing."

- "Rome wasn't built in a day." Our students are not the only ones with short attention spans. Educators want instant results and when they are not forthcoming, they abandon their plans with scarcely a backward look.

- We doubt research and disbelieve evidence. We're often accused of paying more attention to "fad and fashion" than science (Lally & Price, 1997). We're suspicious of data, statistics, and norm-referenced tests. Even when we get the results we want on standardized tests, we're loathe to believe that specific teaching methods, higher expectations, or the materials we used really made a difference. We attribute our results (as my own teachers did when standardized test scores began to rise) to chance or "a good group of kids." Of course, that's because if we're responsible for good news, then we will also be accountable for bad news, a troubling prospect for many educators.

- Programs depend on people, and when key supporters and leaders leave, the energy and momentum that kept a program going may dissipate almost overnight. So, if you think you might be moving on, don't ask your faculty to get behind a massive improvement plan. Your departure will only serve to make them more cynical than they already were about "improvement."

- Constant and ongoing training is necessary to keep a program viable. Every time a new staff member comes aboard, a program will be watered down and less effective unless that individual receives quality training. Educators are notorious for not following through on this commitment, so eventually only a few "old-timers" on a staff are still using a method-ology or approach that was once extraordinarily powerful.

- Lack of supervision and accountability are both major stumbling blocks to successful change. Somebody has to care about these two critical issues, and the building principal is the "go-to" person for "making sure" and "keeping track." If you are not organized, structured, and data driven, find someone to help you who is (e.g., lead teacher, building secretary, or school improvement coordinator). (Latham, 1988, pp. 42-43)

This lengthy introduction filled with reasons why innovations and improvement efforts fail may seem a morbid way to begin, but it's very realistic. Forewarned is forearmed. If you are not prepared to include safeguards into your improvement initiative to help avoid these pitfalls, you are like those who, failing to heed history, are doomed to repeat it.

This chapter is a pivotal one to the book. It explains the "big ideas" you need to understand and internalize before you can lead your school to reading excellence. None of the material in this chapter is revolutionary, but you will find that "doing it" may provide more adventure in your life than the Indiana Jones attraction at Disneyland. Here are the puzzle pieces that you must fit together to create a community of readers in your school:

1. Instructional leadership
2. Shared decision making
3. Planning for change
4. Instructional effectiveness
5. Parental involvement
6. A balanced curriculum
7. Assessment and accountability
8. Five years to make it happen and to see results

Principals Do Make a Difference: Instructional Leadership

What you do on a daily basis in your unique school setting makes a difference in how much and how well the students in your school learn (Hallinger, Bickman, & Davis, 1996). Your ability to successfully respond to the organizational and environmental context in which you work and to create a clear mission for your school directly influences your teachers' expectations for their students and the students' opportunity to learn. This in turn creates a positive effect on student achievement in reading (Hallinger et al., 1996, p. 543). When teachers perceive their principals as strong instructional leaders, students learn (Andrews & Soder, 1987; Heck, Larson, & Marcoulides, 1990; Heck, Marcoulides, & Lang, 1991; Sillins, 1994).

How can you determine if your teachers think you're a strong instructional leader? Ask them! If you want to raise reading achievement in your school, you must begin with yourself. Becoming an instructional leader involves a commitment to the following seven steps (McEwan, 1997b, p. 13):

1. Establish clear instructional goals.
2. Be there for your staff.
3. Create a school culture and climate conducive to learning.
4. Communicate the vision and mission of your school.
5. Set high expectations for your staff.
6. Develop teacher leaders.
7. Maintain positive attitudes toward students, staff, and parents.

Resource D contains a sample Instructional Leadership Behavior Checklist (McEwan, 1997b).

You Can't Do It All on Your Own: Shared Decision Making

Lest you begin to feel totally burdened with the overwhelming responsibility of raising reading achievement in your school, let me assure you that you don't have to do it alone. My training for the principalship included some passing references to participatory management and group decision making, but my job description led me to believe that I was personally responsible for what transpired in my building. Fortunately, I was rescued from that mind-set when the concept of Building Leadership Teams was introduced to our district. After a brief training period, this team of four teachers and I met one afternoon per month charting a course for school improvement and tackling the substantive issues of teaching and learning. My staff members were definitely more committed to implementation when they were involved from the beginning in making important decisions about instruction. After your team is formed, get training to help your group become cohesive and productive (McEwan, 1997a, pp. v-vi).

Now that you're on your way to becoming an outstanding instructional leader and have put together a team of knowledgeable and dedicated teachers who recognize a need for change, your next step is to develop a plan.

Look Before You Leap: Planning for Change

There are many school improvement models, and which one you use is less important than that you actually choose one and stick to it. The National Center to Improve the Tools of Educators (1997a) has developed an excellent handbook that will lead you and your team through four important stages: (a) setting improvement goals, (b) defining the scope of the improvement plan, (c) selecting tools and practices for the improvement plan, and (d) planning and implementation. Many state departments of education also publish School Improvement Plan workbooks (e.g., Connecticut State Department of Education, 1989). We chose just one goal during our first year: Reduce the number of students whose scores in reading fell in the bottom quartile on the Iowa Test of Basic Skills by 10%. Our plan included

1. Increasing our allotted reading instructional time by 50%
2. Implementing a motivational recreational reading program
3. Adding instructional materials to teach phonics more comprehensively in the primary grades
4. Altering our grouping practices
5. Targeting a group of very low students for extra help

Teachers Make a Difference, Too: Instructional Effectiveness

You can have a vibrant and motivated decision-making team, a comprehensive planning document, a fabulous curriculum, and a marvelously supportive parent community but still come up short in reading achievement if your teaching staff doesn't have the instructional expertise to pull it off. The research base detailing the various aspects and nuances of effective instruction although extraordinarily informative is also overwhelming. When one considers the thousands of decisions the skillful teacher makes on a daily basis, be prepared to invest time in training. Ongoing staff development, particularly if you are planning to implement a new curriculum or program, is vital. In addition, consider staff development that also involves strands from the various aspects of effective instruction, which teachers can select according to their needs and interests (see Resource E for reading suggestions to help you). These strands can be taught by master teachers or organized around a self-study cooperative learning group.

The following 12 categories summarize the critical aspects of effective instruction:

1. Instruction is guided by a preplanned curriculum (Venezky & Winfield, 1979). This characteristic speaks to the need for objectives, timelines, and planning in determining what will be done daily in the classroom. If you don't know where you're going, you won't get there.

2. There are high expectations for student learning (Phi Delta Kappa, 1980). Students are not expected to fail, but to learn.

3. Students are carefully oriented to lessons (Stallings, 1979). Students in today's classrooms are frequently at a loss as to what is going on during class. They must be told in advance what is expected of them and be prepared for learning.

4. Instruction is clear and focused (Lortie, 1975). This seems such an obvious statement, but my years of classroom observation have led me to believe otherwise. When I, the experienced former teacher and principal, had no clue about what was being taught, how could students be expected to figure it out?

5. Learning progress is monitored closely (Evertson, 1982). Teachers hold students accountable and use frequent assessments to see if what they're doing is working. They use this information to modify their instruction.

6. When students don't understand, they are retaught (Rosenshine, 1983). When everyone fails the test, the effective teacher figures out what went wrong with his or her teaching and reteaches with an alternative approach. What a novel idea!

7. Class time is used for learning (Stallings, 1980). This is another novel idea. Cut out the assemblies, field trips, fundraisers, and intercom announcements and teach.

8. There are smooth, efficient classroom routines (Brophy, 1979). Efficient classrooms seem to run by themselves with seamless transitions and little "administrivia."

9. The instructional groups formed in the classroom fit instructional needs (Stallings, 1979). This does not mean that ability-based groups formed in kindergarten remain unchanged through high school.

10. Standards for classroom behavior are explicit (Anderson, 1980). Rules, expectations, and consequences are taught to students from day one.

11. Personal interactions between teachers and students are positive (Rutter et al., 1979). Effective teachers really care about their students and demonstrate this care in thousands of brief interactions daily.

12. Incentives and rewards for students are used to promote excellence (Emmer & Evertson, 1981). This practice has come under a lot of fire from the "feel-good" folks, who don't want competition or hurt feelings because everybody isn't a winner. In my opinion and experience, if a student works, he or she will be a winner. When excellence is defined by objective standards and not by peer comparison and the rewards are appropriate for the level of the student, incentives and rewards work. (Northwest Regional Educational Laboratory, 1984, pp. 3-6)

Get Mom and Dad on Your Side: Parental Involvement

Parental involvement and support are crucial to raising reading achievement in your school. In our school, we instituted a simple, no cost, but highly effective parental involvement program that tapped the read-aloud talents of moms and dads. The program was kicked off each year at kindergarten orientation (small-group meetings of parents held by appointment during the 2 days prior to the opening of school) when the teacher explained what we were asking parents to do (read one book aloud to their child every evening). Each school day students could visit the school library and check out a book suitable for reading aloud. Parent volunteers who staffed the media center (along with a full-time librarian and aide) assisted the children in selecting books and in writing their names on the cards if help was needed. The students brought home the books they had checked out, and parents (or older siblings) were expected to read them aloud to their children that evening and return them to school the next day. When students arrived at school, they would write their name (or some facsimile thereof) on a piece of large chart paper thereby letting the teacher know they needed to return a book. The teacher used these sheets as a record to award each child a star on a chart that hung on the wall. By the end of the first quarter, there were very few children who were not taking read-aloud books home almost every day. Parents reported that children literally hounded them if they were remiss about not including a read-aloud session in their evening routine. First- and second-grade teachers continued this practice, which by then was a well-ingrained habit for both students and their parents.

Another way in which we garnered parental support and involvement was through publishing what we called our "I Can Learn" booklet. This booklet set forth the outcomes in reading, writing, and mathematics for all grade levels so parents would know what we as teachers expected their children to learn. We also included a set of teacher expectations (e.g., the teacher is expected to provide quality instruction for all students, hold students accountable for following school rules and completing assignments, and evaluate and commu-nicate student progress to parents and students), as well as expectations for parents and students. This document sent the message to parents that we were serious about learning and that we must all be accountable (teachers, parents, and students) if we were to reach our goals.

I believe that when parents observe the following evidence in your school, they will back you 100%:

- Evidence of children (both their own and others) learning through both formative and published summative evaluations

- Evidence of teaching effectiveness as observed by parents when they are participating in the life of the school as a volunteer or visitor (e.g., frequent planned events that bring parents into classrooms to observe)
- Evidence of educators' desires to make parents a part of the "learning team" through advisory groups, inclusion on the building leadership team, and periodic surveys that ask for parents' input

Know Your ABCs:
Articulated, Balanced Curriculum

I have chaired dozens of curriculum committees as a principal and assistant superintendent for instruction and been a member of many more in my days as a teacher and librarian. In the "olden days," a Reading Committee merely selected a new series. Salespersons delivered copies of all the new books, the committee members inspected them, and then the group voted on its choice. I've been there and done that. It was pretty stultifying to have the principal checking the page numbers in my lesson plan book to make sure I was "where I was supposed to be in the basal reader." But I did learn a lot about reading instruction from those manuals that I'd never learned in college. Nowadays the Reading Committee is called the Language Arts Task Force and its members write outcomes, develop their own curriculum, construct interdisciplinary units, and design performance-based assessments. The results of their multiyear study fill rows of binders in the Professional Library. I've been there and done that too. The folks who are most excited about the binders are those who collaborated with one another to fill them. The teachers in the trenches are often confused about what they are supposed to be doing, lacking either the philosophical underpinnings to understand what reading is all about or the training, maturity, and experience to translate the contents of a binder into exciting instruction. No curriculum, the ostensibly "teacher proof" one or the "teacher invented" one (e.g., the "whole language" and "literature based" curricula), is all-purpose. In fact it is the "either-or" mind-set that is the problem. I like the advice Stanley Pogrow (personal communication, November 17, 1997) gives:

> We all have to stop pretending that we have the answer and start learning from each other. As someone who sees the use of systematic, validated curriculum as critical, I also recognize the need for teacher-inspired and improvised forms of instruction. Why can't we have both, with each coexisting for part of the school day?

This is a balance that we must achieve if reading instruction in our schools is to produce readers.

The materials and methods you (and your staff) select must meet the learning requirements of a wide variety of students as well as satisfy the instructional needs of a continuum of teachers from the newly graduated to the about-to-retire. I believed as a principal and I believe even more strongly now after reviewing the current literature that you must include three components in any reading program you design or choose: (a) phonemic awareness, (b) quality reading materials, and (c) cognitive strategies for reading comprehension.

Students must first be given the tools to enable them to read (phonemic awareness and then decoding). After that, students must be inundated, immersed, and bathed in every conceivable type of reading material (e.g., fiction, nonfiction, poetry, biography, periodicals, and newspapers). My goal as a school librarian was to have my students read (or have read to them in kindergarten and first grade) a book from each major Dewey classification during every school year. I had that same goal for my children as they were growing up. At the same time that students are reading (plus discussing, summarizing, and evaluating) challenging and interesting materials, they must also receive direct instruction in cognitive strategies, those "shortcuts," which when taught to students, will enable them to find solutions and answers for themselves (Jones, Palincsar, Ogle, & Carr, 1987; Pressley et al., 1995). Use of strategies such as webbing, reciprocal teaching (Palincsar & Brown, 1984), and K-W-L (Ogle, 1986) can help students understand and remember what they have read. Over a period of 3 years, our staff identified a group of reading strategies we felt were most critical for our students to use. The staff (including the art, music, and physical education teachers) received training in the use of the strategies, and we used them at every grade level and in every subject as appropriate (e.g., the physical education teacher constructed a "web" on the gymnasium wall illustrating the various units of study and accompanying activities that made up the school year).

These three nonnegotiables of reading all have different instructional emphases, hence the need for teachers who can skillfully move from one instructional mode to another. Some instruction (phonics) is direct and systematic with little opportunity for freelancing and interpretation. It will look the same no matter who is teaching the lesson. To the casual observer, direct instruction can seem mindnumbing and repetitive; that's because the observer already knows the code. To the eager child who desperately wants to learn to read, the process will be as exciting as discovering how to decipher the Rosetta Stone was for Jean-François Champollion.

Other instruction will be creative and freewheeling (e.g., reading novels based on a period in history or a chosen theme, reading plays and performing them, or studying the picture book genre in preparation for writing such a book for kindergarten students). The goal is to inspire a love of reading. There are as many ways to achieve this goal as there are individual children, teachers, and books.

A third kind of instruction will be an inspired combination of both structure and creativity. Teaching individual cognitive strategies requires a prescriptive approach and calls on the teacher to determine which strategies are needed for specific reading assignments as well as for the unique needs of different children. Although cognitive strategies often appear structured and step-by-step, they must be taught and applied in the context of "real reading" situations. This calls for a thorough knowledge of how children learn, an understanding of the thinking process, and the ability to match the strategy to the situation. There are also more technologically based ways to teach cognitive strategies that are a unique combination of structure and creativity.

If you are eager to learn in more detail about the research and expectations for student learning that surround these three components of a balanced curriculum, Chapter 4 provides that information. Only when you are armed with that knowledge and understanding will you and your staff be able to evaluate what you are doing, examine already published materials and programs against these guidelines, and determine if a change is necessary (see Resource F for a listing of materials that may meet your needs as well as a discussion of how to evaluate programs and materials).

What Gets Measured Gets Done: Assessment and Accountability

If you want to lead your school toward reading excellence, you must become an evaluation-minded principal (Nevo, 1991). You must constantly evaluate the teaching effectiveness of your staff, the reading proficiency of your students, and the effectiveness of your programs. Evaluation in each of these areas must be both summative and formative (Scriven, 1967).

> Summative evaluation offers a final determination of the worth of a program or individual's performance in a role. It is not designed to be constructive; rather it is designed to be ultimately judgmental and primarily used by those stakeholders who will make some decision about program or individual continuation. Formative evaluation, on the other hand, is conceptualized as constructive. In both roles, evaluation serves to inform decision making. (Goldring & Rallis, 1993, pp. 96-97)

How will you and your team determine how well your students are learning to read? That decision will have to be made before you launch into your reading improvement plan. If you're going to use a different measure of student achievement than you have presently been using, you will need to administer a pretest to all the students to gather baseline data. I believe that if testing is to be meaningful and helpful to classroom teachers, it must track the performance and progress of each individual student in your school over a several-year period. The tests must be standardized and administered yearly to every student. I am aware of the popularity of performance assessments and believe they are an ideal way for teachers to assess students in the classroom, but my experiences in constructing and administering performance tests at the district level in math and science has led me to agree wholeheartedly with these authors:

> On the basis of the data examined, we are forced to conclude that constructed response items provide less information in more time at greater cost than do multiple choice items. This conclusion is surely discouraging to those who feel that constructed response items are more authentic and hence, in some sense, more useful than multiple-choice items. It should be. (Lukhele, Thissen, & Wainer, 1994, p. 245)

I am also aware of the controversy over testing limited-English-proficient and learning disabled students. Although my state and district offered testing exemptions to these populations, as a principal I wanted to know how effective our efforts were at helping these students join the mainstream. To know that an individual student has made substantial gains in achievement (even if still below grade level) is far more helpful than knowing the composite reading score of the school or a particular grade level. We examined the chronological test scores of each of our students to determine their progress. We were expecting our Target Students (those who were well below grade level) to overcome huge deficits in performance through our interventions, and seeing those results in black and white was tremendously encouraging and motivating to teachers. Gains in reading achievement are made one student at a time. We also disaggregated our data to determine how well we were serving the students in various subpopulations. Overall improvement in reading achievement means nothing if students in the bottom quartile continue to fail.

While you're planning how to summatively evaluate the success of your implementation, don't overlook the importance of formative evaluation, the ongoing monitoring of a program that will help you determine if any students or teachers are "falling through the cracks." The purpose of formative testing is to provide information to the learner and to the teacher about what the learner knows.

Do not hesitate to ask for help with assessment and accountability. Possible sources for technical assistance include (a) a test company consultant who will work with your staff to understand the construction of standardized tests and how they can be used to evaluate your program, (b) a university professor who can be hired to provide the evaluation component of your plan, (c) central office staff who have expertise in this area, or (d) a state department of education consultant.

Take Your Time: The 5-Year Plan

Implementing a new program or curriculum takes time, and if you fast-forward through any critical stages you will fail. As important as vision is, beware of becoming blinded by your own.

The principal who is committed to a particular innovation or philosophy may pursue it in such narrow and self-defeating ways that key teachers will resist the idea until the principal leaves or is transferred. In other cases the principal is "apparently successful" in getting teachers to use the innovation while failing to achieve more basic changes in enabling them to consider alternatives, reflect on their practices, and otherwise improve. (Fullan, 1992, p. 19)

Take the time needed for goal setting, planning, training, implementation, fine-tuning, and evaluation. Consider alternatives and listen to teachers who may have questions or concerns. Teachers typically pass through a variety of stages on their way to successfully implementing a new program; don't push them faster than they can go.

Begin small if you need to. "The objective of evolutionary planning is to capitalize on the 'low risk' quality of smaller-scale innovation to increase certainty. This, in turn, increases motivation, and the possibility of concerted, more 'tightly coupled' action across the school" (Louis & Miles, 1990, p. 211).

The Road to Reading Improvement: The Big Ideas

By way of review, consider once again the big ideas of Chapter 3 that can help you lead your school to reading excellence.

Instructional Leadership

"Schools operated by principals who were perceived by their teachers to be strong instructional leaders exhibited significantly greater gain scores in achievement in reading and mathematics than did schools operated by weak instructional leaders" (Andrews & Soder, 1987, p. 10).

"To lead change, you have to change" (Lynch & Werner, 1992, p. 7).

Shared Decision Making

"It is logical that if you properly combine the judgment of a large number of people, you have a better chance of getting closer to the truth" (Helmer, 1981, p. 81).

"A group of people is not a team. A team is a group of people with a high degree of interdependence geared toward the achievement of a goal or completion of a task. In other words, they agree on a goal and agree that the only way to achieve the goal is to work together" (Parker, 1990, p. 16).

Planning for Change

"There is nothing more difficult to take in hand, more perilous to conduct, or more uncertain in its success, than to take the lead in the introduction of a new order of things" (Machiavelli, 1985, p. 23).

"We strongly recommend that school districts [schools] clearly define their understanding of the desired end result early in the change process" (Harrison, Killion, & Mitchell, 1989, p. 56).

Instructional Effectiveness

"Every school must believe that all children can learn and that all teachers and administrators can help them" (Gauthier, 1980, p. 17).

"There are six basic ways to raise student achievement: (1) change how you teach; (2) change what you teach; (3) change how long you teach; (4) change how you group to teach; (5) change when you teach; and (6) measure what you teach" (McEwan, 1988, p. 34).

Parental Involvement

"When a process makes people feel that they have a voice in matters that affect them, they will have a greater commitment to the overall enterprise and will take greater responsibility for what happens to the enterprise. The absence of such a process ensures that no one feels responsible, that blame will always be directed externally, that adversarialism will be a notable feature of school life" (Sarason, 1990, p. 61).

An Articulated, Balanced Curriculum

"The first and foremost job of elementary school is to teach children to read. The reading program in every school should enable almost every student to be able to read fluently and understand grade-appropriate material; to have read a large number of books, magazines, and other informational texts; to reach high levels of comprehension ability; and to enjoy and learn from reading" (Honig, 1996, p. 1).

Assessment and Accountability

"The purpose of evaluation includes, but goes beyond, accountability. Evaluation looks at programs and personnel and seeks to discover why the programs have had the determined effect and whether the determined effect is one that the school community wants" (Goldring & Rallis, 1993, p. 92).

A 5-Year Plan

"Time is the most valuable thing a man [or a school] can spend" (Theophrastus, 278 B.C.).

What Else Will It Take?

Perhaps you are still in a quandary about the best way to teach reading. That's not surprising considering the controversy that has swirled about reading instruction during the past decades. Chapter 4 will discuss the exciting research findings that seem to point us more clearly than ever to the most effective ways of teaching reading.

The Essential Learnings

What Students Need to Know in Grades K-8

Children are wired for sound, but print is an optional accessory that must be painstakingly bolted on.

Steven Pinker (quoted in McGuinness, 1997, p. ix)

*M*any groups and organizations are telling you how to go about teaching reading in your school: the researchers and scholars who scientifically study the acquisition of reading skills and the best methods to teach them; the professors in teacher education programs who teach beginning teachers to teach reading; the teachers who teach in your school every day; the special ed and Title I teachers who are teaching kids with difficulties; the policymakers in Washington who are deciding where the funding will flow; the state departments of education who prescribe "acceptable curricula"; the companies and organizations who publish materials and promote programs; professional organizations like the National Council of Teachers of English (NCTE), the International Reading Association (IRA), and the Association of Whole Language (TAWL); and finally, the critics who make us feel shallow and stupid or irrational and incensed. If you're not confused, then you've been in hibernation!

Chapter 2 contained a brief history of the "great debate" between phonics and whole language that has consumed all of the above stakeholders in our country's literacy for decades. And if our literacy statistics were terrific, the discussion would be moot. The news is not good, however. The 1992 National Adult Literacy Survey, commissioned by Congress, shows that the United States has an adult literacy rate close to 76%, down from 97% in 1940 (*National Adult Literacy Survey,* 1994).

As a school principal, you need answers today. Where do you turn? Jeanne Chall (1992) suggests three possible sources: "(a) science (the available scientific basis for proposed reforms, as compared with traditional approaches); (b) art (the practice that has worked); and (c) ideology (the values and attitudes that seem to lie behind preferences)." As I suggested earlier, educators are suspicious of science. "Education has suffered because its dominant model for adjudicating disputes is political (with corresponding factions and interest groups) rather than scientific" (Stanovich, 1994, p. 287; see also Stanovich, 1993). And we are ill trained as educators to evaluate research for ourselves, prisoners of a teacher education model that failed to develop our scientific thinking abilities. We and our teachers are hostages to authorities and experts. We're more comfortable with "what works," even if we don't know if it's really working. Rather than asking, "What research do you have to support that what you're doing works?" we ask, "How long would it take to get this up and running in my school?"

The time has come, however, to decide what we're going to do on Monday, and I suggest that science can point the way very clearly. We must come to grips with whether we're going to pay more attention to anecdotal/ethnographic descriptions of how children learn to read or to experimentally verified data. Unfortunately, we cannot do both.

> Although we have a very serious literacy problem, the sources of which are broad and deep in socioeconomic, cultural, and neurological factors, there is much that is in the hands of schools and teachers. . . . The accumulated knowledge on literacy suggests that different aspects of reading be empha- sized at different stages of reading development, and that success at the beginning is essential since it influences not only early reading but reading at subsequent levels, even in high school and college. It demonstrates that a beginning reading program that does not give children knowledge and skills in recognizing and decoding words will have poor results. (Chall, 1992)

My purpose in this chapter is to give you an outline of what research suggests a K-8 reading program should include. Many states and school districts have developed comprehensive documents detailing specific outcomes at every grade level (e.g., California Department of Education, 1996; Texas Alternative Document, 1997), but these can be overwhelming unless you have some "organizing principles" in which to frame them. Our discussion of the following key organizing principles of phonemic awareness and knowledge acquisition in a print-rich environment, immersion in books and print (i.e., reading by doing), and systematic instruction in cognitive/comprehension strategies will be organized in three parts: (a) a brief summary of the major research supporting the principle, (b) the "big" learning outcomes of the principle, and (c) a snapshot of what the classroom and/or school will look like when teaching and learning are going on. Don't forget to consult the Reading Instruction Glossary section in Chapter 2 if you encounter confusing terms.

Direct Systematic Instruction in Phonemic Awareness and Knowledge Acquisition in a Print-Rich Environment

Research

The most comprehensive and significant research to date about how chil- dren learn or do not learn to read has been conducted by the National Institute of Child Health and Human Development. The Web site of the Center for the Future of Teaching and Learning contains a comprehensive synthesis of the research (see Resource C). Spanning over 30 years, the studies are characterized by a scientific rigor and a range of subjects (children of different IQ levels, ethnic groups, and socioeconomic groups) that has been sadly lacking from much of the reading research. Those of you who have come to believe that the only thing that children need from their earliest schooling experience to learn to read is immersion in a print-rich environment and time to "develop" have been sadly misled. They also need direct and systematic instruction in phonemic awareness.

> Research makes clear that children do not learn to read the way they learn to talk. Speech is a natural human capacity, and learning to talk requires little more than exposure and opportunity. In contrast, written language is an artifact, a human invention, and reading is not a skill that can be acquired through immersion alone. Beginning readers benefit from instruction that helps them understand that the words they speak and hear can be represented by written symbols—and that letters and sounds associated with them, when combined and recombined, form words—just as they benefit from experiences that make reading fun. (Council for Exceptional Children, 1996)

Even if you introduce phonics in the context of a whole-language pedagogy, you still won't achieve the results you want because of two heavily used strategies in the whole-language methodology: guessing at unknown words and the use of reader-selected material that may be far too difficult for the student to read independently. A classroom teacher using a phonics-first approach discourages children from guessing the identities of words by assigning stories composed of decodable words selected to provide practice to the students in applying their previously learned phonics knowledge. Decodable texts contain carefully controlled vocabulary for which the student has been fully prepared ahead of time through explicit phonics instruction so that he or she can correctly sound out all the letters.

Following is a summary of the significant research findings that have widespread implications for how the students in your kindergarten and first-grade classes should be learning to read (California Department of Education, 1996; Center for the Future of Teaching and Learning, 1997; Grossen, 1996; National Center to Improve the Tools of Educators, 1997b).

Make children aware of the characteristics of print. Print awareness includes knowing the purpose of reading; the structure of written text; how stories work; what a word is; how words are composed of letters; what spaces signify; and directionality, that is, how print is organized, which necessitates the ability to scan left to right and then sweep diagonally left and one line down (Clay, 1991, pp. 141-154).

Begin teaching phonemic awareness (i.e., the conscious understanding that a spoken word is made up of a sequence of speech sounds) directly and explicitly at an early age (kindergarten). From paleography (the art of deciphering ancient manuscripts) and structural linguistics we have learned that all writing systems are based on the syllable structure of the language for which they were written. From cognitive and educational psychology we have learned that children must be trained to hear the individual sounds (phonemes) of their language. They must be able to disconnect or "unglue" sounds in words to use an alphabetic writing system (McGuinness, 1997, p. xiii). You cannot count on all or even most children developing this awareness naturally; they must be taught. This skill is absolutely essential in learning to read and spell (Ehri, 1986). The lack of phonemic awareness is the most powerful determinant of the likelihood of failure to learn to read. If children cannot hear and manipulate the sounds in spoken words, they will have an extremely difficult time learning how to map those sounds to letters and letter patterns—the essence of decoding (Adams, 1990). Phonemic awareness instruction should begin before instruction in sound-spelling relationships and be continued throughout the teaching of sound-spelling relationships.

The research suggests that phonemic awareness is "a constellation of abilities that centers around the child's emerging and understanding of the segmental structure of the spoken language" (Gough, Larson, & Yopp, 1997). This natural progression of phonemic awareness can and should be taught through preschool, kindergarten, and first grade (Adams, 1990):

1. Rhyme (recognize pairs of rhyming words or produce words that rhyme)
2. Sound oddity tasks (identify words that are the same or different in terms of beginning, middle, or ending sounds)
3. Blending tasks (identify a word when each syllable or phoneme is pronounced separately)
4. Phoneme segmentation (pronounce each separate phoneme in a one-syllable word)
5. Phoneme manipulation (identify the word left when phonemes are added, deleted, or moved)

Teach each sound-spelling correspondence explicitly. One key word in this statement is *explicitly*. It is not adequate to introduce these correspondences in the context of a story and expect a child to figure them out on his or her own. This important aspect of reading instruction cannot be left to chance. The phonemes must be separated from the words for instruction. This can happen only if the teacher isolates each phoneme and each sound for the student. This is an intense listening experience that is best done without the use of key words or pictures. A brief daily lesson that includes the introduction of a new phoneme with practice of those learned earlier is accompanied by the reading of words and stories that use only the letter-phoneme relationships the children know. The other key term in the statement is *sound-spelling*. Most traditional phonics programs use the reverse logic: letters (spelling) to sound. This can be confusing to the beginning reader and often results in more confusion than clarity. Teaching the high-frequency sound-letter relationships early will enable students to experience immediate success when they are given stories that consist of words containing only those relationships that have already been taught.

Teach frequent, highly regular sound-spelling relationships systematically. The key word in this statement is *systematically*. Most sound-spelling programs teach about 40 to 50 relationships, but I am most familiar with the Lindamood-Bell and Phono-Graphix methods (see Chapter 5). These programs begin with one-to-one correspondences (i.e., one sound to one letter), and when these are mastered move on to one-to-many correspondences (one sound to several letters) and then to the "code overlaps" (i.e., those letters that have several different phonemes, or sounds).

Show children exactly how to sound out words through blending the sounds. After children have learned several sound-spelling correspondences, they should then be taught how to blend those sounds into words. They must be shown how to move sequentially from left to right through spellings as they "sound out," or say, the sound for each spelling. Daily practice sessions should include the blending of only the sound-spelling relationships the children have learned to that point. This skill must be overlearned so that it becomes highly accurate and automatic.

Use code-based readers rather than ordinary literature during early instruction. This statement does not mean that children's literature will not be an integral part of the instructional program at preschool, kindergarten, and first grade. Rather, it means that children will not be using ordinary literature for their own reading experiences. A curriculum that encourages guessing may actually hinder reading development. Although prediction is valuable in comprehension for predicting the next event or an outcome of the story, research indicates that it is not useful in word recognition. Children need connected, decodable text to practice the spelling relationships they have learned. The integration of phonics and reading can occur only with the use of decodable text. Children can begin reading decodable text relatively quickly because learning just a few sound-spelling correspondences will enable the reading of dozens of words.

Correct oral reading errors. Whole-language instruction discourages teachers from correcting students who make errors, but children benefit when they receive corrective feedback, regardless of whether the errors influence the meaning of the passage.

Use interesting stories, picture books, poetry, and literature of all kinds to develop knowledge and comprehension. Using a phonics instructional system does not rule out using literature of all types in the classroom. Only the use of these stories as reading material for nonreaders is ruled out. Teacher-read stories can play an important role in building children's oral language comprehension, which ultimately affects their reading comprehension. These story-based activities should be structured to build comprehension and vocabulary skills, not decoding skills. Teachers should read aloud to students several times during the school day and use these opportunities for discussion about text organization (fiction, nonfiction, poetry) and vocabulary development, as well as general knowledge building.

Do both, but don't mix. A common misconception held by many educators is that if they are teaching sound-spelling relationships in the context of real stories, they are teaching phonics. Mixing decoding and comprehension instruction in the same instructional activity is clearly less effective, even when the decoding instruction is fairly structured. When phonics instruction is embedded, it doesn't have the same effect as when it's taught purely and separately (Foorman, Francis, Beeler, Winikates, & Fletcher, in press; Foorman, Francis, Novy, & Liberman, 1991; Torgesen, Wagner, Rashotte, Alexander, & Conway, in press).

Do phonics right. There are hundreds of published phonics programs, and now that the state of California and others have passed legislation regarding phonics instruction there will be dozens more. The "great debate" has polarized the issue and could lead one to mistakenly conclude that "phonics is phonics." To the extent that most phonics programs teach the names and sounds of letters, that is true. They begin with the 26 letters and teach children the sounds that go with them. But there are 43 sounds, and many teachers (and programs) end up confusing kids (and themselves) rather than actually teaching them how to decode (and spell). What the research has shown is that children learn to read most efficiently when they start with the speech sounds (43 of them) and then learn which letter(s) stands for those sounds (Lindamood, Bell, & Lindamood, 1997; McGuinness, 1997) rather than learning the letter names first and then attaching sounds to them. Because the alphabetic code (letters) was developed to match the sounds of language, it only makes sense to start with the sounds first. It would certainly have been handy if each of the 43 English sounds had only one corresponding symbol. But our alphabet has 26 letters (4 of which are wasted), and instead of making up new letters for the leftover sounds, the old letters were reused in some interesting and often inconsistent combinations (McGuinness, 1997, p. 80). The argument that using sounds to teach reading is impossible because of the regional dialects is a specious one (McGuinness, 1997, p. 108). People who speak nonstandard dialects understand the standard dialect perfectly; how else would they understand television, whose announcers and performers take speech lessons to standardize their speech? The biggest problem facing educators is finding programs that do the job right (see Chapter 5 for a discussion of specific remedial programs that can also be adapted for the regular classroom and Resource F for a discussion on choosing materials). Putting an ill-conceived program into the hands of a poorly trained teacher can almost be worse than doing nothing at all. Further complicating the issue is that most children come to kindergarten and/or first grade with two very erroneous assumptions: Letter names are something you sing or chant in an alphabet rhyme that has no relationship to reading, and the way you read is to memorize words by looking at them. Unfortunately, too many kindergarten and first-grade teachers are operating under the same faulty assumptions.

The "Big" Learning Outcomes:
Kindergarten and First Grade

Here are the big learning outcomes that will result from using the research recommendations. A small percentage of students will accomplish the entire list in kindergarten or before (e.g., my daughter, whose story was told in Chapter 2). Those students will obviously need much enrichment and acceleration, but even these early readers can benefit from systematic phonics instruction in terms of their spelling skills and ability to decode multisyllabic words. Most other children will need and use the full 2 years of kindergarten and first grade to "learn to read" (e.g., my son, whose story was also related earlier).

The following set of principles (learning outcomes) prepared for the Learning to Read, Reading to Learn campaign (Council for Exceptional Children, 1996) summarizes what children should know and be able to do as they move through kindergarten and first grade and most definitely by the conclusion of first grade.

1. Have an appreciation of the written word.
2. Have an awareness of printed language.
3. Know the alphabet.
4. Understand the relation of letters and words.
5. Understand that language is made of words, syllables, and phonemes.
6. Know the letter sounds.
7. Decode (sound out) new words.
8. Identify words in print accurately and easily and read them both silently and aloud.
9. Know spelling patterns.
10. Read reflectively and independently. This includes being able to read first-grade material never seen before with fluency and near-complete accuracy, and without needing pictures or having to guess at unfamiliar words. It also includes being able to retell stories read independently.

Classroom Snapshot

Welcome to the ABC Elementary School. Wander down the hallways and peek into a first-grade classroom. To those who have become accustomed to "child-centered classrooms" where small groups of children are looking at books together while the teacher is reading a story aloud to another group in the corner, the atmosphere (only during phonics instruction) will feel foreign. All of the students are sitting in their desks facing the teacher (rather than in the now-typical cooperative groups). There are no books or worksheets on their desks. There is only the teacher and her presentation material on an easel. The teacher points to some words and word fragments. "My turn," she says. She points to individual letters and makes their sounds. "Your turn, get ready," and the children repeat as she slides her pen across the letters. "Fast way," she says, and everyone says the word normally as she slides the pen quickly. Now she chooses another word or set of letters and the process repeats. The pace is furious. The only letup comes when the teacher senses that one or more children are behind the others and are repeating others' responses rather than formulating their own. The repetition, alternation, and sheer speed of the stimuli and responses set up an almost tangible atmosphere in the room, drawing everyone irresistibly into a whirlpool surrounding the teacher. "Too mechanical. It's like an assembly line." Does this program inspire creativity in the students? Not today, it doesn't. But there will be plenty of opportunities for creativity tomorrow, when the child can read effortlessly and devote all of his or her attention to the content rather than to the task of figuring out what the words are (D. Ziffer, personal communication, November 17, 1997).

Immersion in Challenging and Excellent Material: Reading by Doing

Research

P. David Pearson (1993), eminent reading researcher, has suggested a metaphor to describe the emphasis of reading research over the past decade: "the reader as builder." He sees this reader as "an active-meaning constructor, an aggressive processor of language and information who filters the raw materials of reading (the clues left by the author on the printed page) through [his or her] vast reservoir of knowledge to revise continuously a dynamic, ever-emerging model of text meaning" (p. 502). I like this metaphor if it's not carried too far (as have some whole-language constructivists) by claiming that the "content of what is read is unimportant and not very useful in educating our children because most meaning is idiosyncratic and based in the reader's experience" (Honig, 1996, p. 106). Unquestionably, everyone would agree that the purpose of reading is to derive meaning, but there are three significant activities in which students must engage for this to happen.

Students must become voracious readers to become fluent and competent readers. Once students have acquired the ability to decode, the single most important activity in which they can engage is reading. "Reading a lot" is one of the most powerful methods of increasing fluency, vocabulary, and comprehension, and becoming educated about the world (Shany & Biemiller, 1995; Stanovich, 1993). Educators must do whatever they can to encourage students to read a variety of materials (see Chapter 6 for suggestions to increase recreational reading by students). Literature-based classrooms are wonderful to a point, but unless a student intends to major in comparative literature or become a book reviewer for the *New York Times,* the current overemphasis on fiction is misplaced. To be sure, it's fun to read fiction. I have a stack of novels on my bedside table and dip into one each night before bedtime. But I also need to be able to read and comprehend nonfiction for work. Most jobs require all nonfiction reading: documentation, reports, specifications, and policies. There are two main reasons that reading a lot is important: (a) The more students read, the better they comprehend, because the number of words they recognize and understand is increasing by leaps and bounds (Shu, Anderson, & Shang, 1995); and (b) the more students read, the more knowledge they acquire. This in turn helps students to understand even more the next time they read. To that end, students must be required to read a specific number of books each year. The upward spiraling of the "Matthew effect" to which we referred earlier is one of the most powerful forces you can unleash in your school (Stanovich, 1986). The more kids read, the better they get at it. One of my expectations as a principal was that all students would always be in the process of reading a book. I wanted to see this book right on the top of their desks so that when they finished an assignment or had a few free moments, they could just open the book. This was also the book they read during a period of silent reading that went on in every class every day. Teachers were also expected to be reading a book during that period of time. Students (and teachers) didn't have a choice in this matter. I just expected them to read. Whenever they finished a book, they could go to the library to choose another one. The librarian was always available to help them find the right book, one that interested them and one they were able to read independently. And she was keeping track of what and how much they read through our Independent Reading Club. To receive credit for reading the book, students had to "conference" with the librarian. She had an amazing ability to determine if students had indeed read and understood the book, and she engaged them in lively conversations about their reading. Students who achieved the highest honor had their names engraved on a large plaque in the library and were recognized at our quarterly awards assembly.

Students must read challenging and well-written materials. At some point students have to move beyond Goosebumps and Babysitters' Club books. Although these genres certainly serve a purpose in getting the reluctant reader "hooked on books" and I've written a few myself (McEwan, 1991a, 1991b, 1993a, 1993b, 1994), we must raise our expectations for what students read and guide them to the best. There are dozens of suggested reading lists and hundreds of thousands of wonderful books for children (McEwan, in press). Why, then, are teachers in the same school asking their students to read the same novel at four different grade levels? I once spent an entire Language Arts Committee meeting trying to assist teachers in determining "who got *Charlotte's Web*" as if that were the only book in the library. As a former librarian who has fought her share of censorship battles, I am also aware of the difficulty in finding books that please everyone; a community in which I once lived fought a bloody battle over the Impressions reading series. However, reading *Charlotte's Web* at every grade level is not the solution to this problem. This is an important issue that every district and school will have to solve for itself, particularly if instruction is based solely on teacher-chosen trade books and teacher-constructed interdisciplinary units. As a teacher, I believed I should be able to do whatever I wanted to in my classroom if my students were learning. As a principal, I became more rigid in my demands for some curricular standards. When I moved to central office, I began to see the havoc that can be wrought when all are "doing their own thing." A balance must be maintained that assures all children have the opportunity to learn a given set of skills and knowledge and read a wide variety of materials.

Students must be engaged in rigorous discussions of the structure, meaning, and interpretation of the text. Teaching the structure of the text includes practices like pointing out the differences among fiction, nonfiction, and poetry; describing the elements of a story; and guiding students to examine the organization of an expository text while taking notes (Au, 1992; Johnson & Louis, 1987; Lehr, 1991; Ogle, 1986). In addition to learning about the structure of text, students must be expected to personally react and respond to what they read as well as determining what the author's "message" might be (Applebee, 1992, 1994). "Trivial recall questions, unmediated personal responses, and low-level follow-up activities" (Honig, 1996, p. 108) do nothing to serve the reader. Discussion and interpretation are especially critical for late elementary and middle school students where reading and writing around a variety of issues and themes should be taking place on a daily basis.

The "Big" Learning Outcomes: Second Grade Through Eighth Grade

Students will

- Read to learn
- Understand the purposes of reading

- Understand what they read
- Choose to read independently
- Think critically about the meaning, message, and aesthetic value of the text
- Have an ever-increasing knowledge base drawn from their wide readings of literature and informational titles in science, biography, and history

Classroom Snapshot

Take another walk through ABC Elementary School and visit a fifth-grade classroom where students are reading, discussing, and sharing constantly. There is a library stocked with many different kinds of reading materials. There are special places for reading and writing activities. There is a puppet stage and storytelling area that students often use to share their creations with each other and with lower-grade classes. Many of the students have written letters to favorite authors, and their replies are posted on a bulletin board. An after-school Battle of the Books competition is scheduled, and student teams are in small groups surrounded by stacks of books discussing the main ideas and themes of the books on which they'll be quizzed. The students are preparing to produce their own newspaper in the next month and are studying the various parts of a newspaper in anticipation of the local editor's visit to their classroom to make a presentation. There are stacks of newspapers around the room from several different cities in the state. The class has recently helped a local author and her editor "edit" the book she has written culminating in a class visit by the author to read aloud the concluding chapter. There was a heated discussion (in front of the author) about whether the final scene would be really satisfying to readers. This is an environment where students are constantly reading, writing, questioning, and discussing.

Instruction in Vocabulary, Comprehension, and Cognitive Strategies

This third important aspect of reading instruction deals with strategies. We have each developed and used strategies in our own professional preparation. We know the steps involved in writing a research paper, how to remember information needed to pass a qualifying exam, and how to understand and summarize a research study. Each of these projects required a set of different steps and tasks, and we have developed and/or learned methods over time that work for us. These methods are strategies, ways of approaching an intellectual task that help us organize, understand, and remember information. Recent research has suggested that direct instruction in vocabulary and reading comprehension strategies can help students do a better job of organizing, understanding, and remembering what they read. Just as direct instruction in phonics does not mean stacks of worksheets, neither does strategy instruction mean workbook-type assignments (Pearson & Dole, 1987). Although I believe there is much work to be done in this area (both in research and program development) and that well-developed curricula for use by educators are hard to find and sometimes even harder to use, the preliminary findings are very promising.

The three basic types of strategies are

1. Strategies that teachers use when they are presenting material they want students to learn (e.g., the use of mnemonic pictures or devices to help students better remember what is being taught)
2. Strategies that are taught specifically for students to use on their own
3. Strategies that teachers use in their presentations that will, it is hoped, eventually lead to students using them on their own (Pressley et al., 1995, p. 7).

Research

The research with regard to cognitive strategy instruction has taken three routes: (a) single studies of specific strategies generally published in academic journals, (b) the development of packaged comprehensive cognitive strategy programs that have been designed for use with a remedial population but are quickly gaining a foothold in the regular classroom, and (c) school-developed cognitive strategy programs that are site specific.

Individual reading comprehension strategies. There are several major roadblocks to finding effective research-based individual strategies for use in the classroom. Research studies of individual reading strategies are not highly accessible to practitioners, and the information is usually not presented in a teaching format that is immediately usable by the average teacher. In addition, although there are many strategies promoted in the curriculum literature for classroom use, not all have been evaluated in terms of effectiveness.

Here is just a sample of the strategies that have been researched as to effectiveness and widely used by educators with success (see Resource G for a general model of how to teach strategies).

The *story grammar strategy* is especially effective in assisting poor readers with comprehension. Students are taught to ask themselves (and then answer) the following five questions as they read a story: (a) Who is the main character? (b) Where and when did the story take place? (c) What did the main character do? (d) How did the story end? and (e) How did the main character feel? (Short & Ryan, 1984).

The *semantic mapping strategy* helps to improve vocabulary learning (Margosein, Pascarella, & Pflaum, 1982). After students are presented with new vocabulary to be learned, they brainstorm about related vocabulary for each new word. Students construct a graphic by placing the word in the center of a page and then writing lists of related words or phrases at the end of spokes around the word.

The *reciprocal teaching strategy* was one of the earliest to report gains in reading comprehension from teacher-directed strategy instruction (Palincsar & Brown, 1984). Students are taught to use four effective comprehension strategies: prediction, seeking clarification, question generation, and summarization.

Even the introduction of one or two reading strategies in your school, when used consistently across grade levels and curricula, can make a powerful difference in comprehension and reading enjoyment for your students. Cognitive strategy instruction at the middle school level can be especially helpful as adolescents (and their teachers) face a burgeoning body of subject matter for which they are responsible.

Comprehensive cognitive strategy development programs. More indirect but intriguingly elegant approaches to teaching cognitive strategies to students have been suggested by Stanley Pogrow (1997) and Lindamood et al. (1997). These approaches focus on a global development of higher-order thinking skills finding that the development of these skills readily transfers to increased comprehension abilities.

Pogrow has developed a learning drama approach to using computers that combines two of the oldest pedagogical traditions, Socratic dialogue and drama, with the newest forms of technology and learning theory. The program is called HOTS (Higher Order Thinking Skills). Teachers use a variety of commercially available software, but the explicit goals of the software have little to do with the content that is taught or learned and there is virtually no instruction about how to use the software. Students are expected to figure that out on their own using textual clues. Discussions focus instead on ideas that have been designed to develop key thinking skills. Dramatic techniques are used in the lessons to heighten the students' curiosity and motivation. The activity engages the students, and any failure to use content or strategies appropriately has negative consequences for them. Teachers are trained in how to systematically probe student answers in a Socratic manner to produce understanding. (Socratic questioning is teaching by asking questions as opposed to teaching by presenting information.) Although not a cognitive scientist himself, Pogrow's work has harnessed technology in a unique way that may offer robust principles about the types and duration of activities that are needed to help students comprehend and understand what they read.

The Visualizing and Verbalizing for Language Comprehension and Thinking Program by Nanci Bell (1991a, 1991b) guides students to develop a conceptually imaged gestalt (whole) by integrating imagery and language, using specific vocabulary to develop and describe detailed components of mental representations. The visualizing and verbalizing steps begin with given pictures to be described and then extend into word imaging, sentence imaging, sentence-by-sentence, paragraph, and page imaging. Once an imaged gestalt is developed at the sentence-by-sentence level, stimulation for reasoning and higher-order thinking skills is introduced, and the procedures continue with direct application to following directions, vocabulary development, content instruction, study skills, and the ability to organize for writing.

School-developed cognitive strategy programs. The history of the Benchmark School of Philadelphia must command the attention of any school principal considering how to raise reading achievement (Gaskins & Elliot, 1991). Opened with just one class of poor readers in 1970, it has grown under the leadership of Gaskins to a student body of 167 composed entirely of privately funded students whose primary referring problem is poor reading despite average or better intelligence (Gaskins & Elliot, 1991, p. 5). What distinguishes the Benchmark School from the majority of schools has been its development of a research-based cognitive strategy instruction program that pervades every aspect of school life. Working with researchers Richard Anderson (National Academy of Education, Commission on Reading, 1985) and Michael Pressley (1991), the staff of Benchmark has focused on teaching thinking skills while imparting knowledge. Teachers at Benchmark use a three-pronged approach (Gaskins & Elliot, 1991, p. 32): (a) All teachers teach a core group of 17 cognitive strategies for achieving meaning and memory (pp. 54-55); 13 strategies for knowledge production (e.g., composing, problem solving, decision making, and research; pp. 56-57), and 8 metacognitive strategies for use across the curriculum (pp. 58-62); (b) teachers teach strategies specific to domains and situations as the need arises; and (c) two stand-alone courses on learning and thinking are taught that share with students how the mind works to provide them with a rationale for learning the strategies that are being taught in their other classes (pp. 99-120). Other comprehension strategies programs have been developed in two different Maryland school districts (Coley, DePinto, Craig, & Gardner, 1993; Schuder, 1993). I have personally witnessed the power of strategy instruction to improve reading comprehension skills in both my own school and that of my colleague Phyllis O'Connell. She and her staff compiled what they called a "strategy box," trained staff members in how to help students adopt these strategies as part of their academic life, and then watched reading achievement skyrocket in their school (P. O'Connell, personal communication, November 17, 1997).

The "Big" Learning Outcomes: First Grade Through Eighth Grade

- The short-term outcome of cognitive strategy instruction at any level is "deep understanding of the current reading assignment [or learning task]" (Pressley et al., 1995, p. 85).

- The long-term outcome of cognitive strategy instruction is the "internalization and consistently adaptive use of [the strategy] whenever students encounter a demanding text [or learning tasks]" (Pressley et al., 1995, p. 85).

Classroom Snapshot

The classroom is a computer laboratory, and there are no workbooks or worksheets. In fact, students don't even pick up a pencil during today's 45-minute class period (they do on some occasions) until the close of the period when they record their results in a lab notebook. During the first half of the period, the teacher engages the students in a question-and-answer period, probing in accordance with the Socratic method in which the teacher has been specially trained. Although the teacher is following a prescribed dialogue, there is plenty of room for creativity as dramatic techniques are often used to heighten student curiosity and motivation. The discussions are designed to develop metacognition, inference from context, decontextualization, and information synthesis. This is "mind bending" at its best. Following the discussion, students work on their own computer for the rest of the period. The feedback generated from the computer as students work with a variety of software programs provides a continuous flow of information for the student to process, which leads to improvements in his or her personal comprehension and problem solving. The software programs are incidental to the discussion, however, because learning comes from the conversation that focuses on the students "thinking about" what they are doing and why it is or isn't working. As I observe this setting, I am reminded of visiting the video arcade with my grandson. He is manipulating dials and levers, exclaiming over his successes and failures, and I am questioning him as to how he has figured out how to beat this machine. He explains, but I haven't been trained how to listen. In contrast, this teacher is constantly probing the students to articulate their ideas and explain how and why the computer is reacting to their strategies the way it is. This constant pressing of students to examine and explain their strategies increases the sophistication of their language use, both in terms of comprehension and articulation. The increased sophistication of language use enhances students' ability to learn all content. There is no management system in this classroom and no grades. Success is demonstrated by the products generated by the students, their articulation of findings, and the results they record in their lab notebook. The process doesn't seem to be teaching reading comprehension, but remarkably the students who attend the class four times a week during the school year make noticeable progress in all areas of standardized testing, not just reading.

What Else Do You Need?

Your mind is no doubt racing ahead as to the specifics of materials and/or programs to achieve your goal of raising reading achievement. Making this selection is a difficult, time-consuming, and often heated process. Space does not permit a complete discussion of the materials selection and evaluation process in this chapter; however, Resource F contains a sample evaluation system as well as a list of some programs to consider. Additionally, the discussion of programs widely used for remediating poor readers in Chapter 5 will present some options to consider that may well be used for a schoolwide program.

5

Remedial Reading

What to Do When Kids Can't Read

Decoding and comprehension . . . are the two halves of reading. But the two halves are not added together. Reading does not equal the sum of decoding and comprehension, for neither decoding in the absence of comprehension, nor comprehension in the absence of decoding, leads to any amount of reading. A child who cannot decode cannot read; a child who cannot comprehend cannot read either. Literacy—reading ability—can be found only in the presence of both decoding and comprehension. Both skills are necessary; neither is sufficient.

Philip Gough, Wesley Hoover,
and Cynthia Peterson (1996, p. 3)

*I*n my dreamworld, I've designed a school in which we begin with just one preschool class, teach reading right, and then add another preschool class as we move the first cohort on to kindergarten. Although this system of adding one preschool class per year would not totally eliminate the need for remedial help because "real world" classes never move along in a lock-step fashion and many students with problems would "move in" from other places, the scores of poor readers that cause teachers and principals sleepless nights and worrisome days would be almost eliminated. Only in my dreams! In the real world of American public education, most schools are besieged with poor readers for whom time is running out. With each passing school year the "Matthew effect" ensures that these students will fall farther behind while their teachers become more demoralized. Consequently, remedial reading has become a booming business: Sylvan Learning Centers; Title I budgets; Head Start; Reading Recovery; and millions of dollars of books, computer programs, and training sessions. In spite of this massive infusion of funds, we do not seem to be gaining on the problem. More students today are leaving our schools unable to read simple text with understanding than ever before. Where does the solution lie? More money? Increased training? Better research? A different approach? We must find the answers.

The labels applied to kids who cannot read have proliferated faster than our ability to deal with their problems: remedial readers, dyslexic, learning disabled, attention deficit disordered, retarded readers, handicapped readers, laggardly readers, low-achieving readers, problem readers, delayed readers, and readers with an IQ-reading discrepancy. Sometimes we apply these labels in a rather discriminatory fashion. Intelligent children from "good" families are diagnosed with dyslexia, often called the "affliction of geniuses," whereas students who are socially, culturally, and economically deprived find their reading problems laid squarely on the shoulders of their demographics. Whatever their label, however, these students have one of three major problems in varying degrees of intensity:

1. The inability to recognize written words quickly and accurately as a result of a phonemic awareness weakness, that is, dyslexia, or the inability to decode the written word

2. The inability to comprehend exactly what the authors intended to convey, that is, hyperlexia, or the inability to make sense out of what is read

3. The inability to do either, that is, the "garden variety" poor reader (Gough et al., 1996, p. 4)

All of these learning problems need intensive, direct, and systematic instruction.

Two children stand out in my mind as illustrative of these major deficits: Suzi and Jesse. Suzi enrolled in our school at the beginning of third grade. She transferred in from a private school that although highly acclaimed wasn't firing on all cylinders while Suzi was in kindergarten and first grade. She endured a total of five different teachers during her crucial "learning to read" years and consequently never learned to read. Her problem was a relatively simple one: She had never learned to decode and simply guessed her way through every reading passage with which she was confronted. Her problem had nothing at all to do with her comprehension abilities. She was bright and had a better than average general knowledge and vocabulary; she just didn't have a clue about what the words "said." After a comprehensive diagnostic screening and intensive remedial sessions that focused on decoding skills, Suzi was able to catch up. By sixth grade she was a member of the first-place Battle of the Books team and a star reader. The combination of supportive parents, Suzi's high self-esteem, and intensive remedial instruction enabled us to solve Suzi's problem rather quickly.

In contrast, Jesse's problem was much more complex. Jesse was also bright, in fact, extraordinarily gifted. The gap between his ability and performance was over 50 points. In spite of his near-genius IQ and accurate oral decoding skills, Jesse couldn't comprehend what he read. He had been given nearly every label known to modern education by the time he was in fourth grade: gifted, learning disabled, unmotivated, and ADHD. He had been tested, examined, and dissected, but none of our labels or interventions had really served Jesse's educational needs. Although he was a gifted artist and had an amazing gift of gab, his inability to understand what was written on the printed page reduced him to tears more often than not. His initial difficulties in learning to read might have been overcome had we known more and started earlier. But by the time we tried to help Jesse, he exhibited nearly all of the emotional reactions seen in poor readers over time: anger, acting out, fear, depression, withdrawal, and intellectualization. He had developed a whole range of behaviors to protect his dwindling self-esteem. Jesse is a young adult by now; if he graduated from high school that would be a miracle. I still worry about him and wonder what he's doing. I believe that today we know far more about Jesse's problems than we did when he enrolled in our school. I believe there are answers today for Jesse's problem.

These answers are not inexpensive. Remedial teachers handle smaller groups of students, need more advanced training, and require more and sometimes specialized classroom space. Fixing what we have failed to do right in the first place costs big bucks, and that doesn't even count the cost of materials, hardware, and software. Be prepared to have deep pockets when implementing some of the more widely known remedial programs.

The enormous number and variety of programs being used around the country are staggering, and finding ones that actually produce results is a challenge. In the state of Kentucky, only 64 out of about 500 curriculum providers surveyed for a comprehensive guide (Kentucky Department of Education, 1997) could provide evidence that their program produced the desired results (Lawton, 1997). Trying to figure out what might work in your school can be almost as difficult as choosing a mutual fund for your retirement or buying a new car. Actually, it's even more difficult because for those choices you can turn to *Money* magazine or *Consumer Reports*. When it comes to determining how best to help poor readers, we often follow our instincts rather than hard data.

In the remainder of this chapter, I have listed a representative sampling of important and/or well-known methodologies and programs with a brief discussion of the research supporting their effectiveness as well as important questions for consideration that have been raised by other researchers and writers. I have also included one reading series, although not technically a "remedial" program, because of its effectiveness when used in particularly challenging school settings. Principals must carefully examine all claims and counterclaims before committing resources (human and financial) to any program. No program is perfect, and the variables of cost, personnel, and time requirements must be evaluated. Also, keep in mind that many remedial programs can also be considered as a mainstream curriculum, particularly if working in a setting with overwhelming numbers of students who are failing in reading. For ordering information about any of the following programs, see Resource F.

HOTS: The Higher Order Thinking Skills Project

This program is an alternative approach to Title I for Grades 4-6 in which the compensatory activities consist solely of systematically designed higher order thinking activities (Pogrow, 1995). Traditional drill-and-practice activities and content instruction are eliminated. The 2 years of thinking activities are designed to generate gains in basic skills expected from Title I programs while also improving thinking ability and social confidence. By learning how to learn, students are then able to learn content the first time it is taught in the classroom. The program is conducted in a computer lab using a detailed curriculum taught by a teacher specially trained in Socratic dialogue techniques. The teacher is the most critical component of the program, and the program will not be successful without the right teacher. The curriculum is designed in accordance with information-processing theories of cognition. The program operates as a pull-out program for 35 minutes a day, 4 days a week for 2 years. In the first part of the period, the teacher engages students in sophisticated conversations. Students are then given a challenge, which they take to the computer to try to solve. They will later discuss their findings, approaches, and how they know whether their strategy for solving the problem did, or did not, work. HOTS is unique in its ability to produce significant gains in achievement in later grade levels (Darmer, 1995). It is the only remedial program that treats students as though they were gifted and that relies strictly on activities that challenge them intellectually. There is no content remediation or worksheets.

In use for over 15 years as a Title I validated program, schools in which HOTS is used consistently win awards (e.g., West Avenue Elementary School in the Northeast School District in Texas was recognized by the U.S. Department of Education as an exemplary Title I program). In addition, three other HOTS schools in the district received state recognition in 1994 for having at least 70% of the Title I students pass the Texas statewide assessment (Pogrow, 1995).

Lindamood-Bell Learning Processes

In addition to producing the visualizing and verbalizing program for comprehension described in Chapter 4, the Lindamood-Bell group was a pioneer in the development of a pure phonemic awareness program, Auditory Discrimination in Depth (ADD). Although the program was developed for one-on-one treatment in a clinical setting, it is now being refined for use in school settings. I first became acquainted with the program in 1987 when my reading specialist and I investigated its possibilities for use in our school. The logic of the program was impeccable and the research results were impressive. Regrettably, we did not have the human resources to implement the program, but I've never forgotten it, and I commend it to you here as a program that gets results with students of all ages and does it rather quickly (60 hours maximum of one-to-one treatment).

ADD is one of two programs available that is a true linguistic program. Phono-Graphix, described later in the chapter, is the other one. ADD teaches 44 phonemes by a process of discovery, feeling movements of the mouth, and watching these movements in a mirror. The program incorporates a new vocabulary to talk about phonemes (e.g., lip poppers such as /b/, /p/; nasals such as /m/, /n/, /ng/); helps students analyze and track phonemes using colored blocks; and constantly engages the student in Socratic questioning so as to enable the learner to become independent and self-correcting.

The ADD program draws on the sciences of linguistics and speech pathology to develop awareness of the articulatory gestures that produce the phonemes. Rather than identifying some vowels as "long" and some as "short"—which seems very arbitrary because each vowel can be said in a sustained, long way or a brief, short way—the 15 vowel sounds are categorized and classified into just four groups. Second, the oral-motor feedback for consonants and vowels is used to track and verify the identity, number, and order of phonemes in syllables and words (Lindamood et al., 1997, p. 154).

The ADD approach was evaluated as part of the National Institute of Child Health and Human Development study mentioned in Chapter 4. Statistical procedures were used to identify kindergarten students likely to be in the bottom 10% of readers by second grade. The 180 children in the final sample were randomly assigned to one of four methodologies, one of which was the ADD approach (labeled PASP in the study). All the children in the study received 80 minutes per week of one-on-one instruction during a 2 ½-year intervention period (a total of 88 hours of instruction). Data from the final testing indicated that children receiving auditory discrimination in-depth training established a significantly stronger foundation in basic reading skills than children in the other groups (Torgesen, in press). The ADD group also showed the smallest retention rate of children being held back a grade (9%) over time in comparison to 25%, 30%, and 41% for children in the other instructional groups.

Although one would generally think of implementing ADD in early primary grades, the process has also been used with success in upper grades. In one Alaskan school district, a clinic was established for 229 failing students in Grades 3-12 with the average age of the students being 12.4. Each student received an average of 165 hours of treatment over a 6-week period taught by teachers trained by Lindamood-Bell. Learning gains were measured by using a pre- and posttest in the following areas: phonemic awareness, receptive vocabulary, word attack, word spelling, written language comprehension, word recognition, and ability to follow oral directions. Gains were noted in every area measured, with the most dramatic gains occurring in word attack (from the 25th percentile to the 50th) and comprehension (from the 27th percentile to the 41st). Although the results of the research are reported by Lindamood-Bell Learning Processes (1997) and not verified by independent researchers, they are worth considering given the fact that all 229 students treated had heretofore been unable to reach the mastery levels mandated by the district's learning outcomes due to substandard decoding and comprehension skills.

When one is considering a program for teaching all students to decode, ADD offers an exceedingly hopeful prognosis.

Open Court Reading Series

Although it has never been the intention of this book to evaluate basal reading series, one series is mentioned by many principals and reading specialists who have raised reading achievement. Although one author claims the Open Court reading program was designed for middle-class children (Bartlett, 1979, p. 229), it has been used with great success in schools that do not have middle-class demographics. This is not remedial program but a challenging series I would wholeheartedly recommend. The program has a strong phonics component (Breaking the Code), relies primarily on teacher-directed group instruction, and contains outstanding selections for students to read.

Activities and exercises suggested in the Open Court program have two main goals, to place the child in contact with many of the important ideas and achievements of the present and past times and to enlarge his capacity for effective self-expression. The stories and poems in the Readers acquaint him with the best in children's literature; they give him a bird's eye view of his cultural heritage, and they introduce him to significant ideas and concepts. (Open Court Reading Series, 1997 [The Foundation Program, Teachers Guide], p. xiv)

Orton Family of Phonics Methods

The "Orton family" is a constellation of phonics programs that had its genesis in the research and methodology of Dr. Samuel T. Orton, a neurologist who specialized in helping dyslexic and other disabled children (Ellis, 1993). A variety of individuals who trained under Dr. Orton and their disciples have founded and developed a variety of programs. The Orton family of programs (and a handful of other programs that share their multisensory and integrated approach to the teaching of reading, writing, spelling, and speaking) have joined together to form the International Multisensory Structured Language Education Council. Although many of these programs were originally designed to teach children with dyslexia, they have been widely and successfully used in school settings all over the country. Programs with roots in Samuel Orton's work or ties to individuals who originally trained with him include the following: Alphabetic Phonics, the Association Method, the Herman Approach, the Montessori and Sequential Education Approach, the Orton-Gillingham Approach, Project Read, the Slingerland Approach, the Spalding Approach, Starting Over, and the Wilson Approach (Colony, 1995). Resource F contains additional information about these programs. There are dozens of second- and even third-generation programs whose original roots may lie with the original founders or trainers but whose current curriculum and training methodologies vary substantially (e.g., see Riggs Institute Web site in Resource C).

Some critics charge that the Orton family of programs, based as they are on the premise that there is a brain condition called dyslexia, tend to depress teacher expectations and slow down progress. They even question the existence of conditions like dyslexia (McGuinness, 1997, p. 175) despite current research demonstrating differences in the MRIs of individuals with reading difficulties (Lally & Price, 1997).

There are six aspects to the content of the Orton family of programs (McIntyre & Pickering, 1995, p. xii): (a) phonology and phonological awareness (i.e., the study of sounds and the ability to segment words into sounds); (b) sound-symbol association (i.e., knowledge of the various sounds in the English language and their correspondence to the letters and combinations of letters that represent those sounds); (c) syllable instruction (i.e., knowledge about the six basic types of syllables in the English language); (d) morphology (i.e., the study of base words, roots, and affixes); (e) syntax (i.e., the study of grammar, sentence variation, and the mechanics of language); and (f) semantics (i.e., instruction in the comprehension of written language).

The Orton family of programs uses the following principles of instruction (McIntrye & Pickering, 1995, p. xii): (a) Instruction is multisensory using visual, auditory, kinesthetic, and tactile approaches; (b) instruction is systematic and cumulative following the logical order of the language; (c) instruction is direct with no inferential learning being taken for granted; (d) instruction is diagnostic with the teacher having clear responsibility for prescriptive and individualized teaching; and (e) instruction is both synthetic and analytic (i.e., the parts are presented and students are taught how to put them together to make a whole, and/or the whole is presented and students are taught how to break it down into its component parts).

The Spalding method, based on the work of Romalda Bishop Spalding, who trained directly under Samuel Orton (Spalding & Spalding, 1957/1990), has withstood the test of time as to effectiveness and has a broad body of research supporting its effectiveness. Spalding is described as a total language arts approach because it incorporates the following features (North, 1995, p. 217): (a) The teacher provides an exemplary model of pronunciation of speech sounds; (b) students accurately reproduce speech sounds; (c) the teacher shows written symbols with simultaneous presentation of speech sounds; (d) students simultaneously say speech sounds and write symbols; and (e) students blend sounds to produce words, apply pronunciation skills to oral reading, and use strategies to enhance comprehension. "A rather significant and up to date body of data has been assembled showing the indisputable success that many schools are enjoying with the Spalding Method" (Aukerman, 1984, p. 541). S. Farnham-Diggory (1987), director of the Reading Study Center at the University of Delaware, selected the Spalding method for use in the reading clinic there because of its well-developed theories of reading processes, reading development, skill learning, and instruction.

The Gallego School in Tucson, Arizona has been a "Spalding school" for 15 years, a remarkable achievement in a day when innovations appear and vanish overnight. Organized as an alternative back-to-basics school with heavy parental input, the school's students do not come from affluent homes. Rather, 60% of the students receive free lunch and over 80% are Hispanic. The school has, however, consistently ranked at or above the national and state averages on a standardized test and ranks first among all the schools in its district, outdistancing the district average by 20+ points at Grades 3, 4, and 5. With all of its teachers trained at the Spalding Education Foundation in Phoenix (see Resource F for further information), the school enjoys a remarkable consistency of instruction and purpose (R. Oakes, personal communication, November 27, 1997).

Phono-Graphix

This is the second of the two programs (Lindamood-Bell is the other) that offer pure training in phonemic awareness, phoneme segmenting, and blending. The program eliminates letter names and all exercises or language that conflict with the logic of the code or that add an unnecessary memory load. It teaches 43 phonemes of the English alphabet code as represented by approximately 100 letters or letter combinations. There are three levels. Level 1 teaches the basic code (i.e., the correspondence of one sound to one letter with no digraphs). Skills training covers phoneme analysis, segmenting, blending, reading, and spelling. These skills are mastered in simple three-sound words and words containing consonant clusters. Level 2 is the advanced code level and includes consonant and vowel digraphs followed by phonemes with multiple spellings (i.e., one sound to many letters) as well as code overlaps (i.e., the 21 vowel letter patterns that overlap more than one word sound: the letters *ou* stand for five phonemes). Level 3 teaches multisyllable words up to five syllables, and students are taught to build words by syllable and to decode by syllable. The curriculum materials are hands-on. The motto of Phono-Graphix is "Teach nothing that must be discarded later on" (McGuinness, 1997, p. 317). Phono-Graphix was developed to teach every important skill necessary to read, write, and spell, and to teach them as rapidly as possible. Some clients reach their goals in as few as 12 hours. Although the methodology was developed in the Read America Clinic in Orlando, Florida for use by individuals (both adults and children) who had not had success in learning to read in school, the system has been adapted for use with small groups in the school setting. In one first-grade classroom, a teacher who had been trained in the Phono-Graphix method implemented the program 4 to 5 days per week in groups of four to nine students ages 6 through 10 years (McGuinness, McGuinness, & McGuinness, 1996). During the treatment period (8 months), the students received no formal reading instruction in the classroom but instead engaged in sustained silent reading and other language arts activities. Pre- and posttests were administered including the Woodcock Reading Mastery word identification subtest and word attack subtest, a blending test, a segmenting test, the phonemes manipulation test, and the code knowledge test. The average pretest score on the word attack subtest of the Woodcock was first grade–seventh month. The average posttest score on the word attack was seventh grade–second month, reflecting an average gain of over 5 years. The lack of a control group and the disturbing absence of any kind of comprehension-strategy-building activities in the regular classroom during the treatment period notwithstanding, the preliminary testing results are promising. More research is definitely needed but when phonemic awareness and fluent decoding of authentic text are what you want to teach (and they should definitely be a priority goal in kindergarten and first grade), this program is well worth a closer look. A parent manual has also been developed (McGuinness & McGuinness, 1998).

Reading Mastery–DISTAR

This program has been most commonly used in special education instruction during the past 20 years. Originally developed by Wesley Becker and Siegfried Engelmann (Engelmann & Bruner, 1983) as a program for disadvantaged children, it has been adapted for the regular classroom and is now published by SRA/McGraw Hill. DISTAR uses face-to-face instruction by a teacher using carefully scripted daily lessons in decoding skills.

Project Follow-Through was a massive, federally funded educational experiment of the late 1960s and early 1970s designed to find the best ways to teach disadvantaged children. Models of programs in three different categories were evaluated: basic skills models, cognitive/conceptual skills models, and affective skills models. One of the programs included in the basic skills models was the DISTAR program, also known as the direct instruction model. This model was shown by Project Follow-Through to work across various sites and types of children, producing positive achievement benefits not only in basic skills (the focus of its teaching) but also in higher-order cognitive and affective skills (Stebbins, St. Pierre, & Proper, 1977). Evaluation of 1,000 Direct Instruction graduates showed that they were still ahead of their cohorts in their senior year of high school. Despite its success, there are aspects of the program that disturb some educators. Bartlett (1979) hypothesized that children trained with DISTAR may have a difficult time moving from the coded text (marked long and short vowels, silent letters in long vowels written in tiny type, and dots printed below each letter that is sounded). In real text these cues are missing and this could be problematic. Bartlett's conclusions, however, are not based on her observations of children but rather on her theoretical literacy perspective and bias. DISTAR's highly scripted lessons, emphasis on rote learning, and highly teacher-centered focus are also disturbing to some contemporary educators. The program is nearly three decades old, and for those who find that new is better, DISTAR may seem dated. However, when one evaluates the overall effectiveness of DISTAR based on experimental research, it works. DISTAR does have some gaps (based on what we now know about the importance of phonemic awareness) in its instructional sequence that limit its effectiveness, namely, its lack of training in segmenting sounds and other types of phoneme analysis, and requires extensive training of staff.

Reading Recovery

Reading Recovery is one of the most well known and popular remediation programs in the United States. It has literally swept the country. Although Reading Recovery itself is now copyrighted and there is a carefully screened and very lengthy teacher training process, there are many variations on this theme developed by those who didn't want to commit the time and money the "real" Reading Recovery takes. I was personally "taken in" by the seductive claims of one Reading Recovery clone while an assistant superintendent for instruction. I made my decision based on the fact that this program/methodology was developed in New Zealand where literacy was the highest of any developed nation in the world. If everyone in New Zealand can read, I reasoned, this must be a fabulous program. We'd better have it right away. I did not take the time to investigate the truth of the matter and accepted the enthusiastic recommendation of a colleague. I have since wised up, done my homework, and discovered that New Zealand's reputation for being the "best" is based on a 1970 international reading survey of 15 countries in which their 14- and 18-year-olds ranked top. Literacy rates in New Zealand today are plummeting, and there is national concern over the reasons (Chamberlain, 1993, p. 68). In a country of 3.4 million, close to 20% of the population is illiterate (p. 75).

Reading Recovery, a tutoring program aimed at the bottom 10% to 20% of first graders, has been called a "huge ambulance at the bottom of the cliff" by New Zealand educator Tom Nicholson (quoted in Chamberlain, 1993, p. 69), who wonders why the country isn't doing it right in the first place rather than waiting until children fail (between 30% and 50% of the children in New Zealand are eligible for Reading Recovery at the end of first grade). The program was developed by reading expert Marie Clay in the early 1970s, exported to Ohio in 1984, and is also well-ensconced in the United Kingdom. The National Reading Recovery Center, located on the Ohio State University Campus, is directed by education professors Carol Lyons, Gay Su Pinnell, and Diane DeFord. Students are pulled out of their classrooms for half an hour of one-on-one tutoring. Reading Recovery has the following characteristics in common with whole language (Stahl, 1995): Both approaches uses only whole books; skills are taught in the context of real reading and writing, not in isolation; the reader is viewed as orchestrating a variety of strategies to identify words and does not focus on one strategy (e.g., phonics) to the detriment of others; and readers use predictable texts and invented spelling as integral parts of instruction. Lessons typically include seven activities in the following order: (a) rereading of two or more familiar books; (b) independent reading of the previous day's new book from which the teacher takes a running record or miscue analysis; (c) letter identification; (d) writing a story the child has composed, which includes emphasis on hearing sounds in words (phonemic awareness component); (e) reassembling a cut-up story; (f) introducing a new book; and (g) reading the new book. In spite of the glowing reports that word of mouth has spread about Reading Recovery, three unbiased analyses (Carpenter, 1996; Grossen, Coulter, & Ruggles, 1996; Spear-Swerling & Sternberg, 1996) of the Reading Recovery research findings (Batelle Consulting, 1995; Pinnell, Lyons, & DeFord, 1988) identify major questions and problems regarding both its effectiveness peda-gogically and its cost-effectiveness. Before you consider implementing Reading Recovery, please read one or more of these reviews in full. Here is a brief summary of what one of the evaluators found (Grossen et al., 1996):

- The data reporting system is flawed (half of the data on children eligible for the program was omitted from the final analyses).

- The criteria for what constitutes success varies from class to class and school to school (students need only to achieve at the average level of their class, which in a low-income area can be as low as the 20th percentile on a nationally normed test).

- Achievement levels overall in a school are not affected by Reading Recovery (Hiebert, 1994; Pinnell & Lyons, 1995). Both proponents and critics of Reading Recovery agree on this point, and this fact alone is enough to make one question allocating the time and money Reading Recovery requires.

- Children who are successful in Reading Recovery are often not success-ful later on. When they are returned to their classrooms, they do not make the same progress that average children in the class make.

- Reading Recovery is very expensive.

- Children who are not likely to be successful in Reading Recovery are not even accepted into the program thereby eliminating the possibility of having to include low scores.

- If a child does not complete the Reading Recovery program for any reason, his or her scores are not included in the success rate calculation.

- Only a certain percentage of students in each school are served regard-less of the overall performance of the total student population. There-fore, in low-income schools with a heavy concentration of nonreaders, many students will not be served.

- Under Reading Recovery's definition of success (i.e., ability to read graded books at a certain level), the children who exit the program can rarely read authentic text. The books used in testing are predictable text, which is much easier.

In comparisons with other reading interventions, the claims made by Reading Recovery for a high success rate with problem readers are not upheld. Rather, programs that provide explicit systematic phonics with extensive practice in reading decodable text are more effective with Title I children than a Reading Recovery approach (Foorman et al., in press; Wasik & Slavin, 1993).

Success for All

Success for All (SFA) was developed by Robert Slavin and his group (Slavin, Madden, Dolan, & Wasik, 1996) at Johns Hopkins University in response to a request from the Baltimore, Maryland public schools to develop a program for children (prekindergarten through sixth grade) who were failing. The program is based on the philosophy that all can learn to read, and its ultimate goal is to do away with special education. We used a forerunner of the SFA reading program at our school in the late 1980s. Cooperative Integrated Reading Instruction (CIRC) combined whole-group instruction with cooperative groups with a strong emphasis on writing and discussion to enhance reading comprehension and vocabulary development. Implementation of SFA is schoolwide, and reading groups are made up of children from three grade levels (a much different approach from that of CIRC). During the reading period, the entire school regroups in different classrooms based on each child's reading skill (Joplin Plan). Reading specialists teach the reading classes and during the rest of the day work in tutorial sessions with students who need extra help. The reading program in kindergarten and first grade includes phonemic awareness training plus some phonics and whole language. There is a strong emphasis on comprehension and story analysis. If the sample lessons included in a recently published report are representative of most of the teaching, however, teachers encourage students to do a great deal of guessing when they come to words they don't know (Slavin et al., 1996, pp. 82-87).

In a report presented to the conference of the American Educational Research Association, Slavin and Madden (1995) reported that

> the results of evaluations of 19 Success for All schools in nine districts in eight states clearly show (1) that the program increases student reading performance, (2) that SFA students learned significantly more than matched control students, and (3) that there were unequivocal benefits for Success for All students.

Recently published research offers an excellent opportunity to evaluate the program's success at meeting these goals. Although SFA was clearly more effective than the curriculum being taught in the control classrooms (Slavin et al., 1996, pp. 200-204), the performance of those students in the lowest 25% is quite disturbing. When one examines their longitudinal test data over a 5-year period, it becomes clear that the "eclectic" approach of SFA is not eliminating reading problems the way its designers had hoped. For example, competent readers generally have nearly identical scores on subtests of word attack (phonetic nonsense words) and word identification skills. Less-competent readers who are depending on a sight vocabulary and using visual memory as their primary strategy usually have a large discrepancy. Although the fifth-grade SFA students when considered as a group have fairly similar word attack and word identification grade equivalents (4.50 and 4.79, respectively), the students in the lowest 25% score 1 year higher when reading real words than when reading nonsense words (2.15 and 3.12). And even though the lowest 25% of the fifth-grade SFA students are performing above the controls' grade equivalents (1.51 and 2.24), their scores are still abysmally low. Although Slavin's work in Baltimore is better than anything going on in the other classrooms of the system, there are clearly some missing components in its early instructional program that if in place would truly ensure success for all.

What's a Principal to Do?

Here's my best advice as you set out to find programs that will work for your school:

- Read and evaluate the research. Always read about both sides of an issue.
- Talk to practitioners who have implemented a program (over a number of years). People, in the beginning, are always enthusiastic about what they are doing. Does a program have what it takes to become institutionalized, or is extinction more likely?
- Consult with your staff, especially those who have been successfully teaching beginning reading for a period of time.
- Implement a small pilot study (and include a control group) so you have a personal sense of how something will work in your setting before you launch into full-scale implementation.
- Take the time to examine all the program components and have them evaluated by experienced teachers.

6

Thirty-Plus Things You Can Do Tomorrow to Raise Reading Achievement

> The more elements of good parenting, good teaching, and good schooling children experience, the greater the likelihood that they will achieve their potential as readers.
>
> *Becoming a Nation of Readers*
> *(National Academy of Education,*
> *Commission on Reading, 1985, p. 117)*

Principals can implement a wide variety of relatively simple and inexpensive activities, policies, and programs in their schools to improve reading achievement. Following are 30-plus such things. Some are easier than others, but each will contribute in some way to the overall goal: raising reading achievement. These are time-tested ideas that I have implemented during my career as a teacher, librarian, principal, and assistant superintendent, but I must give credit for them to the wonderful colleagues with whom I worked. These individuals always came to planning meetings brimming over with creativity and energy.

1. Articulate Your Curriculum

Do a simple survey of your reading curriculum and find out if it is articulated (i.e., joined together). Articulated means the following:

- The mastery of certain key skills and concepts is required at some point (i.e., there are expectations that students will achieve certain benchmarks at critical grade levels, e.g., third, sixth, and eighth).

- All the teachers in the school are using the same vocabulary, employing similar methods of instruction, and teaching related cognitive strategies schoolwide so that students can build on their learnings from grade to grade.
- Teachers are not spending so much time reviewing that they never introduce anything new.
- Teachers are not requiring students to read the same books at more than one grade level (students are, of course, always free to reread old favorites during recreational reading).
- Teachers have a clear understanding of what students are expected to learn in their grade level as well as all others and can explain to parents how what they are doing relates to the learning continuum.
- All teachers at the same grade level coordinate their instructional efforts to ensure that each student (e.g., in fourth or fifth grade) gets comparable reading instruction (time, type, quality).

2. Reduce Class Size

Reducing class size at upper grade levels is nice but not as essential as doing it at kindergarten and first grade. Teachers at these grade levels need as much one-to-one time with students as possible, and reducing class size will increase their opportunities.

3. Release Your staff

One of our most effective programs over time was the periodic release of teachers individually or by grade level from their classroom responsibilities for one-half day. Teachers can do a variety of things, any one of which has the potential to raise achievement: talk about each of their students' progress with the principal, reading specialist, and school psychologist; meet with a reading consultant to learn a new reading strategy to implement in their classroom; or plan a unit of study that would involve all classrooms at a grade level. On some occasions, one or more of the teachers would train their colleagues in a new strategy.

4. Read Aloud Every Day

Every teacher in every classroom should be reading aloud to every student every day. In kindergarten and first-grade classrooms, reading aloud will occur more frequently and be the centerpiece of a comprehension lesson. In upper grades, the read-aloud period might be less structured. Care must be taken to coordinate the books that are read aloud. Although it's fun to hear a favorite book read more than once, we should do all we can to expose our students to a wide variety of literature.

5. Give Reading Homework

If your school does not have a homework plan, it should. This plan details how much and what kind of homework students at various grade levels will be expected to do. Silent reading at home was always a part of our students' homework responsibilities. Parents of students who were not able to read independently were expected to read aloud to their children to fulfill this requirement of the homework assignment.

6. Turn Off the TV and Turn On to Books

Organize a reading incentive program that focuses on using free time to read rather than to watch TV. One family I know decided to get rid of their TV altogether after participating in a program to turn off their TV for 1 week. Exceptions to the TV boycott might be news and weather programs.

7. Use Volunteer Readers in Your School

Arthur Tannebaum, a New York executive, created Everybody Wins in 1989. The program organizes adult volunteers to spend 1 school lunch hour a week with an individual child to read aloud. You can find out more about this program by writing Everybody Wins, Dept. P., 165 E. 56th St., New York, NY 10022 (Greer, 1995, pp. 20-21). We held a Community Read-Aloud each year and invited many different community leaders and parents into our school to read their favorite book aloud and talk about the importance of reading in their work. There is an organization called Rolling Readers, California's largest nonprofit children's literacy organization, that assigns volunteers to schools (or other locations like homeless shelters) to read aloud. Three times a year they have a book giveaway. Find an ambitious person (or business) in your community who is looking for a way to make a difference in the lives of kids and ask him or her to organize a volunteer reading program for you.

8. Have Students Read a Lot

At the Benchmark School (Gaskins & Elliot, 1991, p. 8), students choose from a library of color-coded books, which makes it possible for to them select books at their independent reading levels. Gaskins, the school's director, has found that giving students manageable books to read leads to increased proficiency. Students follow up their reading with an individual book conference held with a teacher or teacher assistant. Students should always have a book for independent reading on top of their desk, and whenever they have completed their work or have a few extra minutes they should be reading.

9. Use Sustained Silent Reading (SSR) or Drop Everything and Read (DER) Programs

These are two of the more common acronyms for programs that have all students in a school reading silently for a certain period of time every day. I believe this practice is absolutely essential if you want your reading achievement to increase. In some schools, everyone stops to read at the same time. We found this schedule to be too suffocating and artificial, and we gave everyone the flexibility to schedule the read-aloud period whenever they wanted to.

10. Check It Out

The school librarian or media specialist should be an expert in matching books and kids. He or she should work closely with teachers to be aware of special needs a student may have. My librarian had an ongoing reading program in which students conferenced with her after reading a book and were then given credit toward eventually being honored as a Newberry Reader. Their names were engraved on a permanent plaque in the library.

11. Hold a Biography Day

Motivating students to read something other than fiction is sometimes a challenge. We held a yearly Biography Day for students in fifth grade. They chose a biography and read it, did additional research in other books to find information on their individual, and then prepared a monologue assuming the identity of their famous person. The culminating event was a presentation to parents and the rest of the student body in which every student dressed in costume and gave his or her monologue. This activity integrated reading, writing, and speaking while being highly motivating.

12. Create Classroom Libraries and Reading Corners

Although we had an open-door policy in our library (students could check out books any time they wanted to), there were many occasions when teachers wanted to supervise the book selection process. That's when a classroom library comes in handy. Make sure that teachers have budgets to purchase paperback books for their classrooms and encourage them to establish reading corners where students can relax while they read.

13. Join Reading Is Fundamental

Although membership in Reading Is Fundamental (RIF) is not open to everyone, being a part of this organization will enable you to offer free books to students several times during the school year. We coordinated our book give-aways with various reading themes. For one of our giveaways, we held a parade to celebrate reading, and every student and teacher dressed as one of their favorite book characters. Our "old-fashioned" parade, led off by the high school marching band, wound through the main street of downtown where we were greeted by waving businesspersons and eager parents. Our destination was a park adjacent to the public library where we had erected a platform and microphone. We invited the mayor, the director of the library, and Ronald McDonald to share what reading meant to them. Other giveaway themes revolved around the rain forest, our ancestors and the good old days, and a hot air balloon launch. You can find out more about the RIF foundation by writing to Reading Is Fundamental, 600 Maryland Ave., S.W., Suite 600, Washington, DC 20024-2569; phone: 202-287-3220. Even if you can't join RIF, find a benefactor in your community to help you give away free books to students.

14. Implement Reading Incentive Programs

Each year our school planned a reading incentive program with a different theme. Sometimes students were given tickets for every half hour of reading time they put in (time had to be verified by teachers or parents). One year we held a drawing for prizes (e.g., bicycle, VCR, cassette recorders, certificates to local restaurants). Another year those whose names were drawn went with me to a Chicago Cubs baseball game. One year we charted our reading progress on a giant map of the United States as we "jogged" across America. The culmination of that event was seeing me jog around the school building in my bathing suit (three times for every class that met their reading goal. There are as many different reading incentive ideas as there are faculty members in a school. We had a different committee to plan the incentive each year to avoid burnout. Keep your plan realistic and easy to manage.

15. Have a Battle of the Books

This program was coordinated by the children's librarian at our local public library. She and her staff selected 40 books each year. Teams of fourth-, fifth-, and sixth-grade students were formed (five students each). Each team member was responsible for reading eight of the books. The program began in the fall to permit time for students to read the books, and then in-school battles were held to determine the all-school winner. An all-city battle was held at the public library, and winners received medals. We required every student to participate on a team and held mock battles in our library after school for those who wanted to practice. Students made up the questions to ask each other, which really helped improve reading comprehension.

16. Invite an Author

There's nothing like the presence of a "real" author to motivate students to read. I have spent many a day at schools as the "author in residence," and I can tell from the detailed questions students ask about my books that they have read them thoughtfully and carefully. Try to find a local author so your expenses won't be too high. Hold a book fair in conjunction with the author's visit to sell his or her books as well as others.

17. Set Real Reading Goals

Decide as a faculty that you will raise reading achievement and set a measurable goal (e.g., reduce the number of students in the bottom quartile by 10%). What gets measured gets done. Share that goal with the superintendent and ask him or her what contributions central office can make to reaching this goal. Share the goal with parents and ask them what they will be willing to do to help. When we reached our goal, my superintendent took the faculty out for a party.

18. Buy Books

Find ways to allocate funds to your school library for book purchases. Encourage the parent organization in your school to raise funds for books. Suggest that families donate a book (preselected by the librarian) in honor of birthdays. Make sure the librarian is buying books in a wide variety of categories. I once worked with a librarian who loved the Old West. She had a notable collection in this area but didn't buy any easy books for beginning readers.

19. Read to the Principal

Invite beginning readers to share their new skills with you. Give them a button or sticker to show they read aloud to you.

20. Read Aloud Yourself

Your visible presence in classrooms reading books sends a powerful message to your staff and students. Schedule at least half a dozen read-aloud sessions every week.

21. Have a Family Reading Night

Hold a family reading night in which activities for the evening are centered around books and reading. Invite an author to speak. Have books for sale. Give demonstrations of storytelling and poetry reading. To close the evening, turn down the lights and read a bedtime story. Serve hot chocolate and cookies.

22. Broadcast Fireside Read-Alouds

Use your local-access cable station to broadcast a read-aloud session. One principal I know taped his read-aloud from a cozy chair in front of a blazing (artificial) fire. You'll find yourself becoming a celebrity as your students say they heard you reading aloud on TV. Give extra points to students who can tell you about the story you read aloud.

23. Use America Reads

President Clinton thinks he thought of reading tutors in the school himself, but schools everywhere have been tapping into the volunteer force for decades. However, if legislation will get us more volunteers, I'm all for it. Use this initiative to gain leverage with community and business leaders in your area.

24. Hold a Reading Roundtable

Hold a reading roundtable instead of a regular faculty meeting. Most faculty meetings are a boring waste of time anyhow. Put all of the announcements into memo form and use your valuable time to discuss reading instruction. Ask someone to demonstrate a strategy they've found successful in their classroom. Invite students to talk about their experiences learning to read. Ask all the teachers to talk about a book they've been reading recently (see if that doesn't shake up some teachers).

25. Observe Reading Instruction Daily

Observe reading instruction at some grade level every single day of the school year. There is no substitute for knowing what is going on in the classroom. You should be aware of the students who are having difficulties. You should regularly affirm those teachers who are effective and regularly counsel with those who are having difficulties. Your mere presence in the classroom even if you do or say nothing will affect achievement in a positive way (Andrews & Soder, 1987).

26. Evaluate Reading Instruction

When you are writing those dreaded teacher evaluations, make specific references to reading instruction. Commend those who are doing a good job. Suggest ways of improving for those who are unsuccessful. What you highlight in the evaluation process will become important to teachers.

27. Read About Reading, Talk About Reading, Do Reading

Conduct your own self-study program about reading instruction. Become an expert. Tutor a child to find out how challenging reading instruction can be. Teach your teachers. Talk to your teachers. Engage them in meaningful dialogue and discussion about the reading process. Ask questions wherever you go. Find out if teachers have reasons for doing what they are doing.

28. Keep a Principal's List

I knew all the students in my school who were Target Students (i.e., students whose achievement was below grade level). I observed how and what they were doing when I was in classrooms. I made sure I asked teachers about their progress. These were often students for whom no one else was either able or willing to act as an advocate. When teachers knew that I cared, their expectations for these students increased.

29. Publish Your Students' Books and Your Own, Too

Every student should have the opportunity to write and publish books that will eventually be bound and placed in the school library. Find parent volunteers who are willing to start an in-house book publishing company. I began writing while I was a principal and used my moonlighting career to give me leverage in the classroom. Students delighted in talking to me about the books I had written, and I frequently gave presentations on writing and reading in the classrooms.

30. Write About Reading

I began writing a column in our local newspaper while I was a principal. This gave me a public forum in which to discuss the importance of reading as well as other school issues. But you don't need the local newspaper to spread the word. Write about reading in your school newsletter. Publish a list of books for parents to read aloud to their children.

31. Regroup

If you're still using the traditional three reading groups at every grade level, consider doing some regrouping. Research shows that teachers have lower expectations for students in the bottom group. Use grouping as an instructional tool, not as a "cast in concrete," self-fulfilling prophecy.

32. Train Reading Assistants

Train a cadre of parents and pay them a minimal hourly rate to act as reading assistants. We used a state reading grant to fund this project and trained parents in how to work with children in reading a story.

33. Implement Kindergarten Checkout

Get kids in the reading habit on the first day they enroll in your school. Every kindergarten student should have the opportunity to check out a new book from the school library every day and take it home to be read aloud. Children can actually "train" their parents to read aloud to them every evening if the teacher will encourage and keep track of each child's reading.

34. Make More Time for Reading

Reallocate instructional time to spend more of it in reading instruction and reading-related activities. While you're increasing allocated time, evaluate whether your students have a high rate of time on task, that is, time in which they are experiencing success in their learning tasks. Spending more time on reading for a student who doesn't have the tools to read is meaningless.

You will no doubt add dozens of additional ideas to this list. Share them with your colleagues. Publish an article in your state principals' association journal.

Afterword

Writing *The Principal's Guide to Raising Reading Achievement* has been an energizing experience for me. There has never been, in my opinion, a better time to be about the business of raising reading achievement. There are promising research results, public interest and support for literacy that goes all the way to the White House, and an enormous job to be done. I hope that you will rise to the challenge and lead your school to reading excellence.

If you have questions, comments, or success stories to share, please contact me at emcewan@azstarnet.com.

Resource A

What Do You Believe About Reading?

Teaching of Reading Survey

If you answered yes to every question on the survey, you're a whole-language enthusiast from head to toe. But you should at least consider this statement:

> In the final analysis, none of the whole language principles are supported by any evidence, not by the historical record, not by "structural linguistics" which made it possible to decipher writing systems and understand how they work, not by any scientific research on how children actually learn to read. (McGuinness, 1997, p. 55)

If you answered no to all of the questions in the survey, you're most unusual and are probably considered to be an old-fashioned "fuddy-duddy" by your colleagues. If you answered yes to some of the questions and no to others, you're confused about just what you do believe and what you should be doing in your school. That can make for what I call "instructional dissonance," a state of total confusion and lack of focus in the classroom. You need more information and understanding to construct a personal belief structure before you can effectively lead your school to increased reading achievement.

Here are the original quotations from which the survey statements were developed:

1. "Children must develop reading strategies by and for themselves" (Weaver, 1988, p. 178).

2. "It is easier for a reader to remember the unique appearance and pronunciation of a whole word like 'photograph' than to remember the unique pronunciations of meaningless syllables and spelling units" (Smith, 1985b, p. 146).

3. "One word in five can be completely eliminated from most English texts with scarcely any effect on its overall comprehensibility" (Smith, 1973, p. 79).

4. "English is spelled so unpredictably that there is no way of predicting when a particular spelling correspondence applies" (Smith, 1985a, p. 53).

5. "Children can develop and use an intuitive knowledge of letter-sound correspondences [without] any phonics instruction [or] without deliberate instruction from adults" (Weaver, 1980, p. 86).

6. "Sounding out a word is a cumbersome, time-consuming, and unnecessary activity" (Weaver, 1980, p. 86).

7. "Matching letters with sounds is a flat-earth view of the world, one that rejects modern science about reading" (Goodman, 1986, p. 37).

8. "There is nothing unique about reading, either visually or as far as language is concerned" (Smith, 1986, p. 188).

Reprinted by permission of *The Annals of Dyslexia*, International Society of Dyslexia, Baltimore, Maryland.

Resource B

Recommended Reading List

Adams, M. J. (1990). *Beginning to read: Thinking and learning about print.* Cambridge: MIT Press.

This well-written and eminently readable book summarizes many of the critical issues that have swirled about the "great debate" as well as updating Jeanne Chall's Learning to Read: The Great Debate. *Adams comes down on the side of a balanced approach to reading instruction, which manages to offend just about everybody who wants "their way" to be first, best, and only.*

Balmuth, M. (1982). *The roots of phonics.* New York: McGraw-Hill.

This is a straightforward volume of history and scholarship. If you want to understand at what point in history we lost confidence in the alphabetic code and the roles that Horace Mann and John Dewey played in its demise, check this book out.

Chall, J. (1983). *Learning to read: The great debate* (2nd ed.). New York: McGraw-Hill.

Don't even bother with the first edition. The second edition is basically the same except for an updated summary. You will need to read this book as background (cultural literacy for educators, if you will) to understand all of the subsequent discussion and argument that has ensued.

Flesch, R. (1955). *Why Johnny can't read.* New York: Harper & Row.
Flesch, R. (1981). *Why Johnny still can't read: A new look at the scandal of our schools.* New York: Harper & Row.

Both of Flesch's books are somewhat inflammatory and may raise your blood pressure, but they are instructive in understanding some of the political issues involved. They will definitely cause you to think.

Goodman, K. (1986). *What's whole about whole language?* New York: Scholastic Press.
Goodman, K. (1993). *Phonics phacts.* New York: Scholastic Press.

Goodman, whole-language guru, has written widely and his breezy, conversational style makes for interesting reading. Don't take someone else's word for what "whole language" is; don't even think you already understand what it is—read what one of the founding fathers has to say.

Honig, B. (1996). *Teaching our children to read: The role of skills in a comprehensive reading program.* Thousand Oaks, CA: Corwin.

Honig is on a mission to help educators remain research based while combining the best of both worlds—"a literature-driven and language-rich language arts program that fosters deep engagement with a text and a comprehensive, organized skill development program" (p. vii). This is a readable book and an excellent desk resource.

Juel, C. (1994). *Learning to read and write in one elementary school.* New York: Springer-Verlag.

This well-written book is an outstanding ethnographic study describing what it takes to bring the children of the poor to reading competency. The author believes that first-grade reading comprehension is almost always a matter of word recognition.

Routman, R. (1996). *Literacy at the crossroads: Crucial talk about reading, writing, and other teaching dilemmas.* Portsmouth, NH: Heinemann.

Routman is first a teacher and because of her grounding in the realities and practicalities of making something work on a daily basis brings a measure of common sense to the discussion/debate. Although Routman is a strong advocate for whole-language instruction, she also has a clear understanding of where it went wrong and what can be done to fix it. She is honest and plain-speaking.

Smith, F. (1985). *Reading without nonsense: Making sense of reading.* New York: Teachers College Press.

Smith is a psycholinguist and, along with Ken Goodman, one of the guiding lights of the whole-language movement. If you hate research studies and citations, you'll love reading this book by Smith. He offers scarcely more than a page of suggestions for further reading and not a single footnote. If you want his technical discussions and supporting arguments, check out Understanding Reading *(1982), New York: Holt, Rinehart & Winston.*

Spalding, R. B., & Spalding, W. T. (1990). *The writing road to reading: The Spalding method of phonics for teaching speech, writing & reading* (4th ed., rev.). New York: William Morrow.

If you don't really understand "phonemic awareness" and haven't a clue about what "phonics" really is, find this updated and revised classic from 1957 and read it. You'll be intrigued by what you find, I promise.

Resource C

Web Sites

*T*he following Web sites offer some fascinating places to go for information, discussion, and thought-provoking ideas about reading instruction. Although each of the sites was operable and provided the indicated information at time of publication, my apologies for any changes that may have occurred since then.

America Read Challenge is an initiative of the federal government under the Clinton administration that calls on all Americans to support teachers and help ensure that every American child can read well and independently by the end of third grade. This site describes the legislation, answers questions, and provides research and publication information.

http://www.ed.gov/inits/americareads/index.html

Arizona Parents for Traditional Education provides information on reading research and illustrates what activist parents are doing on the Web to change the way reading is taught. The group is based in "Ken Goodman country," which makes for an interesting perspective on the whole-language and phonics debate.

http://www.theriver.com/public/tucson_parents_edu_forum/

The **Center for the Future of Teaching and Learning** in Santa Cruz, California contains an excellent synthesis of research on reading from the National Institute of Child Health and Human Development.

http://www.cftl.org/

This **ERIC** Web site has a wealth of research information, bibliographies, and special reports about phonics and its use in the classroom.

http://www.indiana.edu/eric_rec/ieo/bibs/phonics.html

The **HOTS** Web site provides information about a program for Title I and LD students in Grades 4-8. Implementation requirements and costs are described. Published articles and evaluation results are also included. Interested individuals can order free materials about the program. The site also provides information about the new UltraHOTS schoolwide model for Grades 1-7 that combines HOTS with other state-of-the-art curricula to bring problem-solving activities to all students in all content areas in an enjoyable and practical way.

http://www.hots.org

The **I Can Read** site is an example of what one concerned parent is doing in his area to respond to the lack of phonics instruction in the public schools. There are a variety of interesting links on this site as well as information about Direct Instruction.

http://projectpro.com/icanread.htm

The **International Dyslexia Association** (IDA) was formerly known as the Orton Dyslexia Society. It is an international, nonprofit, scientific, and educational organization dedicated to the study and treatment of dyslexia. The IDA was first established nearly 50 years ago to continue the pioneering work of Dr. Samuel T. Orton, who was one of the first to identify dyslexia and its remediation.

http://www.interdys.org/

The **International Reading Association,** whose mission is to promote literacy, has a variety of information on its site as well as a link to its on-line journal.

http://www.reading.org/

The **Lindamood-Bell Learning Processes** site offers information on ADD (Auditory Discrimination in Depth) and the Visualizing-Verbalizing (reading comprehension) components of their program.

http://www.lblp.com

The **National Center for Educational Statistics** collects and reports statistics and information showing the condition and progress of education in the United States and other nations to promote and accelerate the improvement of American education. You can access a variety of studies and reports. If you like statistics, this is the place for you.

http://nces.ed.gov/

The **National Council of Teachers of English** includes teachers of English at all levels. The organization works to increase the effectiveness of instruction of English, language, and literature and to provide information and aids to teachers involved in formulating curriculum objectives.

http://www.ncte.org/

The **National Right to Read Foundation** has as its mission to return phonics and good literature to every school in the nation. There are a variety of interesting links on this site as well as materials for purchase.

http://www.jwor.com/nrrf.htm

Parents for Improved Education in Fairfax County is another example of how concerned parents are questioning the state of reading instruction. There is an especially interesting analysis of the three reading programs used in the Fairfax County (Virginia) public schools.

http://www.geocities.com/capitolhill/9155/

The **Riggs Institute** is a nonprofit organization that promotes the teaching of phonics.

http://www.riggsinst.org

The **Spalding Education Foundation** was founded by Romalda Spalding to ensure that her teaching methodologies and philosophies might be used by the widest number of educators. The site provides a description of the Spalding method and supporting research. Visitors to the Web site are also able to view a catalog and order materials.

http://www.spalding.org

Special Education Resources on the Internet (SERI) is a collection of Internet-accessible information resources of interest to those involved in the fields related to special education.

http://www.hood.edu/seri/

The **Texas Alternative Document** (TAD) is a set of language arts curriculum standards written by a group of educators who objected to the "official" version, the Texas Essential Knowledge and Skills (TEKS), which can be viewed at http://www.tea.state.tx.us/teks. Both documents are comprehensive and worth examining as you consider what you want your students to know when they leave your school.

http://www.htcomp.net/tad

The **University of Oregon** site has links to the National Center to Improve the Tools of Educators including *A Handbook for Creating Smart Schools* (http://darkwing.uoregon.edu/ncite/smart.htm), a summary of research on achievement grouping and tracking (http://darkwing.uoregon.edu/ncite/smart.htm), and complete research results of Project Follow-Through (http://darkwing.uoregon.edu/adiep/ft/).

http://darkwing.uoregon.edu

Resource D

Instructional Leadership Behavior Checklist

Instructional Leadership Behavioral Checklist

	Never	Seldom	Sometimes	Usually	Always
Indicator 1.1:	1	2	3	4	5

Involves teachers in developing and implementing school instructional goals and objectives.

Indicator 1.2:	1	2	3	4	5

Incorporates the designated state and/or system curriculum in the development of instructional programs.

Indicator 1.3:	1	2	3	4	5

Ensures that school and classroom activities are consistent with school instructional goals and objectives.

Indicator 1.4:	1	2	3	4	5

Evaluates progress toward instructional goals and objectives.

Indicator 2.1:	1	2	3	4	5

Works with teachers to improve the instructional program in their classrooms consistent with student needs.

Indicator 2.2:	1	2	3	4	5

Bases instructional program development on sound research and practice.

Indicator 2.3:	1	2	3	4	5

Applies appropriate formative procedures for evaluating the instructional program.

	Never	Seldom	Sometimes	Usually	Always
Indicator 3.1:	1	2	3	4	5

Establishes high expectations for student achievement, which are directly communicated to students, teachers, and parents.

	Never	Seldom	Sometimes	Usually	Always
Indicator 3.2:	1	2	3	4	5

Establishes clear rules and expectations for the use of time allocated to instruction and monitors the effective use of classroom time.

	Never	Seldom	Sometimes	Usually	Always
Indicator 3.3:	1	2	3	4	5

Establishes, implements, and evaluates with teachers and students (as appropriate) procedures and codes for handling and correcting discipline problems.

	Never	Seldom	Sometimes	Usually	Always
Indicator 4.1:	1	2	3	4	5

Provides for systematic two-way communication with staff regarding the ongoing objectives and goals of the school.

	Never	Seldom	Sometimes	Usually	Always
Indicator 4.2:	1	2	3	4	5

Establishes, supports, and implements activities that communicate to students the value and meaning of learning.

	Never	Seldom	Sometimes	Usually	Always
Indicator 4.3:	1	2	3	4	5

Develops and uses communication channels with parents for the purpose of setting forth school objectives.

	Never	Seldom	Sometimes	Usually	Always
Indicator 5.1:	1	2	3	4	5

Assists teachers in setting personal and professional goals related to the improvement of school instruction and monitors the successful completion of these goals.

	Never	Seldom	Sometimes	Usually	Always
Indicator 5.2:	1	2	3	4	5

Makes regular classroom observations in all classrooms, both informal and formal.

	Never	Seldom	Sometimes	Usually	Always
Indicator 5.3:	1	2	3	4	5

Engages in preplanning of classroom observations.

	Never	Seldom	Sometimes	Usually	Always
Indicator 5.4:	1	2	3	4	5

Engages in postobservation conferences that focus on the improvement of instruction.

	Never	Seldom	Sometimes	Usually	Always
Indicator 5.5:	1	2	3	4	5

Provides thorough, defensible, and insightful evaluations, making recommendations for personal and professional growth goals according to individual needs.

	Never	Seldom	Sometimes	Usually	Always
Indicator 5.6:	1	2	3	4	5

Engages in direct teaching in the classroom.

	Never	Seldom	Sometimes	Usually	Always
Indicator 6.1:	1	2	3	4	5

Schedules, plans, or facilitates regular meetings of all types (planning, problem solving, decision making, or inservice/training) between teachers to address instructional issues.

	Never	Seldom	Sometimes	Usually	Always
	1	2	3	4	5

Indicator 6.2:

Provides opportunities for and training in collaboration, shared decision making, coaching, mentoring, curriculum development, and making presentations.

	Never	Seldom	Sometimes	Usually	Always
Indicator 6.3:	1	2	3	4	5

Provides motivation and resources for faculty members to engage in professional growth activities.

	Never	Seldom	Sometimes	Usually	Always
Indicator 7.1:	1	2	3	4	5

Serves as an advocate of students and communicates with them regarding aspects of their school life.

	Never	Seldom	Sometimes	Usually	Always
Indicator 7.2:	1	2	3	4	5

Encourages open communication among staff members and maintains respect for differences of opinion.

	Never	Seldom	Sometimes	Usually	Always
Indicator 7.3:	1	2	3	4	5

Demonstrates concern and openness in the consideration of teacher, parents, and/or student problems and participates in the resolution of such problems where appropriate.

	Never	Seldom	Sometimes	Usually	Always
Indicator 7.4:	1	2	3	4	5

Models appropriate human relations skills.

	Never	Seldom	Sometimes	Usually	Always
Indicator 7.5:	1	2	3	4	5

Develops and maintains high morale.

	Never	Seldom	Sometimes	Usually	Always
Indicator 7.6:	1	2	3	4	5

Systematically collects and responds to staff and student concerns.

	Never	Seldom	Sometimes	Usually	Always
Indicator 7.7:	1	2	3	4	5

Acknowledges appropriately the earned achievements of others.

SOURCE: Reprinted from *Seven Steps to Effective Instructional Leadership,* by Elaine K. McEwan, pp. 180-181. Copyright © 1997, Corwin Press, Inc.

Resource E

Instructional Effectiveness Resource List

Resources to Promote Teacher Effectiveness

One of the most productive staff development programs implemented in our district included teacher training in Madeline Hunter's model of instruction. Although Hunter's model is outstanding, there are others that also will serve you well (e.g., Rosenshine, 1983). Hunter's books can be used as the basis for staff development strands or courses for beginning teachers who have not been exposed to this material in their preservice education.

The following books are Hunter classics, listed with their original dates of publication. The entire series was recently acquired and reprinted by Corwin Press.

Hunter, M. (1967). *Motivation theory for teachers*. Thousand Oaks, CA: Corwin.

Hunter, M. (1967). *Retention theory for teachers*. Thousand Oaks, CA: Corwin.

Hunter, M. (1967). *Teach more—Faster!* Thousand Oaks, CA: Corwin.

Hunter, M. (1971). *Teach for transfer*. Thousand Oaks, CA: Corwin.

Hunter, M. (1976). *Improved instruction*. Thousand Oaks, CA: Corwin.

Hunter, M. (1982). *Mastery teaching: Increasing instructional effectiveness in elementary, secondary schools, colleges and universities*. Thousand Oaks, CA: Corwin.

Hunter, M. (1990). *Discipline that develops self-discipline*. Thousand Oaks, CA: Corwin.

Hunter, M. (with Breit, S.). (1976). *Aide-ing in education*. Thousand Oaks, CA: Corwin.

Hunter, M. C. (with Carlson, P. V.). (1977). *Improving your child's behavior*. Thousand Oaks, CA: Corwin.

Hunter, M. (with Lawrence, G.). (1978). *Parent-teacher conferencing*. Thousand Oaks, CA: Corwin.

Hunter, M. (with Russell, D.). (1989). *Mastering coaching and supervision*. Thousand Oaks, CA: Corwin.

Here are some other classic resources to share with your teachers:

Brophy, J. (1979). Teacher behavior and student learning. *Educational Leadership, 37,* 33-38.

Kerman, S. (1979). Teacher expectations and student achievement. *Phi Delta Kappan, 60,* 716-718.

Levin, T., & Long, R. (1981). *Effective instruction.* Alexandria, VA: Association for Supervision and Curriculum Development.

Rosenshine, B. (1983, March). Teaching functions in instructional programs. *Elementary School Journal,* pp. 335-351.

Sparks, G., & Sparks, D. (1984). *Effective teaching for higher achievement.* Alexandria, VA: Association for Supervision and Curriculum Development.

Squires, D. A., et al. (1984). *Effective schools and classrooms: A research-based perspective.* Alexandria, VA: Association for Supervision and Curriculum Development.

Resource F

Choosing Materials

Phonics-Based Reading Programs

When you call to request a catalog from any of these phonics-based reading programs, be sure to request current research regarding the effectiveness of the program in both clinical and school settings. This is, of course, only a partial listing of available phonics-based reading programs. Many of these use a multisensory approach and include a variety of audio and video components. Some also provide teacher training programs. An important aspect of evaluating any phonics program is to determine the match between the phonic generalizations taught and the opportunity students have to use and practice those generalizations in their independent reading. If the phonics program does not come with readers, you and your staff must then provide a wide variety of excellent decodable materials from another source for students to read. "The types of words which appear in beginning reading texts may well exert a more powerful influence in shaping children's word identification strategies than the method of reading instruction" (Juel & Roper/Schneider, 1985, p. 151).

Action Reading
(800) 378-1046

Alphabetic Phonics (Texas Scottish
   Rite Hospital for Children,
   Dyslexia Therapy)
2222 Welborn St.
Dallas, TX 75219-3993
(214) 559-7425
Connie Burkhalter

Chall/Popp Reading
(800) 233-0759

Discover Intensive Phonics for
   Yourself
(800) 333-0054

Herman Method Institute
4700 Tyrone Ave.
Sherman Oaks, CA 91423
(818) 784-9566
Renee Herman

Home Quest Learning Labs
(800) 767-7409

Jolly Phonics
(800) 488-2665

Language Tune-Up Kit
(800) 334-7344

Lindamood-Bell Learning Processes
416 Higuera St.
San Luis Obispo, CA 93401
(805) 541-3836
(800) 233-1819
Pat Lindamood
Nanci Bell

Merrill Linguistics (K-3)
(800) 772-4543

Modern Curriculum Press
(800) 321-3106

Open Court (Breaking the Code)
(800) 722-4543

Orton-Gillingham Academy
1322 7th St. S.W.
Rochester, MN 55902
(507) 288-5271
Sharon O'C. Rome

Phonics Pathways & Pyramids
(800) 468-8911

Phono-Graphix/Read America Inc.
P.O. Box 1246
Mount Dora, FL 32757
(407) 332-9144
(800) 732-3868
Carmen McGuinness
Geoffrey McGuinness

Primary Phonics/Explode the Code
(800) 225-5750

Project Read/Language Circle
P.O. Box 20631
Bloomington, MN 55420
(612) 884-4880
Victoria Greene
Mary Lee Enfield

Reading Mastery/Rainbow Edition
(800) 772-4543

Saxon Phonics
(800) 284-7019

Sing, Spell, Read, and Write
(800) 321-8322

Slingerland Institute
One Bellevue Center
411 108th Ave. NE 230
Bellevue, WA 98004
(206) 453-1190
Clara McCulloch

Spalding Education Foundation
2814 W. Bell Rd., Suite 1405
Phoenix, AZ 85023
(602) 866-7801

Total Reading
(800) 358-7323

Wilson Language Training
162 West Main St.
Milbury, MA 01527
(508) 865-5699
Barbara A. Wilson
(800) 899-8454

Zoo Phonics
(800) 622-8104

Comprehension and/or Other Types of Programs

HOTS Program
Education Innovations
2302 E. Speedway Blvd., Suite 114
Tucson, AZ 85719
(520) 795-2143
Stanley Pogrow

Success for All
Center for Research on the Education
    of Students Placed at Risk
Johns Hopkins University
Baltimore, MD
(410) 516-8000
Robert E. Slavin

Considerations in Evaluating Basal Reading Series

The amount of decodable text that is provided for students to read will have a powerful impact on their feelings of success. Keep in mind that even when meaning-based programs (i.e., whole-language programs) include instruction in phonics in their programs, there are few opportunities for the students to practice applying these principles in connected reading. Decodable text consists of words in which every sound-letter correspondence in the word has been taught before the child reads the word. Dr. Patrick Groff, professor of education emeritus, San Diego State University, suggests the following questions be used when evaluating beginning reading texts:

1. What percentage of the words in the stories of the texts of the program that are presented for the first time to pupils (at the various grade levels) are decodable? That is, what percentage of these new words have children been fully prepared, ahead of time, to decode by sounding out all of their letters? The standard for a decodable word is that the child is prepared ahead of time to deal with or process each one of the speech sound/letter combinations . . . each one of them . . . not some of them . . . not a few of them . . . not most of them . . . but each one of them!

2. How much teaching time in the texts (at the various grade levels) is scheduled for instruction of each of the letter-speech sound correspondences (i.e., each bit of phonics information)? What percentage of each reading lesson (Grades K-2) is devoted to systematic, explicit phonics instruction?

3. How many different lessons are devoted to the instruction of each letter-speech sound correspondence? In how many different lessons is each correspondence taught?

4. How often are letter-speech sound correspondences taught for the first time after new words involving them have already appeared in stories?

5. How frequently in the texts are teachers advised to tell children to guess at the identities of words (both new ones and previously introduced) through the use of sentence context cues? (It is imperative that beginning readers be weaned away from this practice and taught to decode words using phonics skills.)

6. Do texts advise teachers to designate as "sight words" some new words that are introduced? If so, what is the definition given of sight words? How many of the so-called sight words have letters that children have been prepared previously to decode by sounding them out? (This is a critical issue because beginning readers readily can infer the correct pronunciation of a word if they can use phonics skills to produce its approximate pronunciation.)

7. Do the texts train children to become consciously aware of the speech sounds in a spoken word (to have phonemic awareness of it) before they are taught to associate these speech sounds with the letters in the written version of the word? What percentage of the texts' scheduled teaching time in kindergarten and Grade 1 is devoted to developing phonemic awareness in a direct and systematic way?

8. Do the texts advise teachers to require pupils immediately to spell correctly each of the words they have learned to decode? (This is a crucial matter because pupils' correct spelling of words greatly reinforces their ability to read them on later occasions.)

9. How soon in the instruction provided by the texts is special teaching arranged for pupils who are relatively slow in attaining phonics and spelling skills? How often are review lessons on phonics information provided? (It is essential that slow learners get extra help and that all pupils overlearn phonics skills to the point that they readily can be put to use when needed.)

10. How often do the texts provide for formal testing and recording of the progress that students make in learning to apply phonics information accurately, spell correctly, understand the various meanings of the words, and understand precisely what authors intended to convey? Is this testing done frequently and thoroughly enough?

SOURCE: Evaluation questions are reprinted permission of Patrick Groff.

Resource G

How to Teach Cognitive Strategies

General Model of How to Teach Strategies

Teach a few strategies at a time, intensively and extensively, as part of the ongoing curriculum; in the beginning, teach only one at a time, until students are familiar with the "idea" of strategy use.

1. Model and explain each new strategy.

2. Model again and reexplain strategies in ways that are sensitive to aspects of strategy use that are not well understood. (The students are constructing their understanding of the strategy, refining the understanding a little bit at a time.)

3. Explain to students where and when to use strategies, although students will also discover such metacognitive information as they use strategies.

4. Provide plenty of practice, using strategies for as many appropriate tasks as possible. Such practice increases proficient execution of the strategy, knowledge of how to adapt it, and knowledge of when to use it.

5. Encourage students to monitor how they are doing when they are using strategies.

6. Encourage continued use of and generalization of strategies, for example, by reminding students through the school day about when they could apply strategies they are learning about.

7. Increase students' motivation to use strategies by heightening student awareness that they are acquiring valuable skills that are at the heart of competent functioning with learning tasks.

8. Emphasize reflective processing rather than speedy processing; do all possible to eliminate high anxiety in students, encourage students to shield themselves from distraction so they can attend to the academic task.

SOURCE: Reprinted, by permission of the publisher, from *Cognitive Strategy Instruction That Really Improves Children's Academic Performance*, by Michael Pressley, Vera Woloshyn, and Associates (1995), Cambridge, MA: Brookline Books.

References

Adams, M. J. (1990). *Beginning to read: Thinking and learning about print.* Cambridge: MIT Press.

Anderson, L. M. (1980). Dimensions in classroom management derived from recent research. *Journal of Curriculum Studies, 12,* 343-356.

Andrews, R., & Soder, R. (1987, March). Principal leadership and student achievement. *Educational Leadership, 44,* 9-11.

Applebee, A. N. (1992). The background for reform: Rethinking literature instruction. In J. A. Langer (Ed.), *Literature instruction: A focus on student response* (pp. 1-17). Urbana, IL: National Council of Teachers of English.

Applebee, A. N. (1994). Toward thoughtful curriculum: Fostering discipline-based conversation. *English Journal, 83*(2), 45-52.

Athans, M. (1997, November 3). Young readers left to struggle. *Baltimore Sun* [On-line]. Available: http://www.sunspot.net/

Au, K. H. (1992). Constructing the theme of a story. *Language Arts, 69,* 106-111.

Aukerman, R. C. (1984). *Approaches to beginning reading.* New York: John Wiley.

Bartlett, E. J. (1979). Curriculum, concepts of literacy, and social class. In L. B. Resnick & P. A. Weaver (Eds.), *Theory and practice of early reading* (Vol. 2, pp. 229-242). Hillsdale, NJ: Lawrence Erlbaum.

Batelle Consulting. (1995). *Longitudinal study of Reading Recovery: 1990-91 through 1993-94.* Columbus: Ohio Department of Education.

Bell, N. (1991a). Gestalt imagery: A critical factor in language comprehension. *Annals of Dyslexia, 41,* 246-260.

Bell, N. (1991b). *Visualizing and verbalizing for language comprehension and thinking.* Paso Robles, CA: Academy of Reading.

Bloom, B. (1980). *The state of research on selected alterable variables in education.* Chicago: University of Chicago Department of Education.

Brooks, J. G., & Brooks, M. G. (1993). *In search of understanding: The case for contructivist classrooms.* Alexandria, VA: Association for Supervision and Curriculum Development.

Brophy, J. (1979). Teacher behavior and its effects. *Journal of Educational Psychology, 71,* 733-750.

California Department of Education. (1996). *Teaching reading: A balanced, comprehensive approach to teaching reading in prekindergarten through grade three* [On-line]. Sacramento: California Department of Education. Available: http://goldmine.cde.ca.gov/cilbranch/teachrd.htm

Carbo, M. (1987). Reading style research: What works isn't always phonics. *Phi Delta Kappan, 68*, 431-435.

Carbo, M. (1988). Debunking the great phonics myth. *Phi Delta Kappan, 70*, 226-240.

Carbo, M. (1989). An evaluation of Jeanne Chall's response to "Debunking the Great Phonics Myth." *Phi Delta Kappan, 71*, 152-157.

Carbo, M. (1996). Whole language or phonics? Use both. *Education Digest, 61*, 60-64.

Carpenter, B. (Ed.). (1996). *Reading Recovery task force report*. San Diego, CA: San Diego County Office of Education.

Center for the Future of Teaching and Learning. (1997). *Summary of seminar sponsored by the California Education Policy Seminar and the California State University Institute for Education Reform* [On-line]. Available: http://www.cftl.org/

Chall, J. (1983). *Learning to read: The great debate*. New York: McGraw-Hill. (Original work published 1967)

Chall, J. (1989). Learning to read: The great debate 20 years later—A response to "Debunking the Great Phonics Myth." *Phi Delta Kappan, 70*, 521-537.

Chall, J. (1992, Winter). The new reading debates: Evidence from science, art, and ideology. *Teachers College Record* [On-line]. Available: ehost@epnet.com

Chamberlain, J. (1993, June). Our illiteracy: Reading the writing on the wall. *North and South Magazine–Auckland, New Zealand*, pp. 67-76.

Chomsky, C. (1976). After decoding: What? *Language Arts, 53*, 288-296, 314.

Church, S. M. (1996). *The future of whole language: Reconstruction or self-destruction?* Portsmouth, NH: Heinemann.

Clay, M. M. (1991). *Becoming literate: The construction of inner control*. Portsmouth, NH: Heinemann.

Coleman, J. (1966). *Equality of educational opportunity*. Washington, DC: U.S. Department of Health, Education and Welfare, Office of Education.

Coles, G. S. (1997, April 2). Phonics findings discounted as part of flawed research [Letter to the editor]. *Education Week*, p. 45.

Coley, J. D., DePinto, T., Craig, S., & Gardner, R. (1993). From college to classroom: Three teachers; accounts of their adaptations of reciprocal teaching. *Elementary School Journal, 94*, 255-266.

Collins, J. (1997, October 27). How Johnny should read. *Time*, pp. 78-81.

Colony, B. (1995). History of Orton-based multisensory structured language methods. In C. W. McIntyre & J. S. Pickering (Eds.), *Clinical studies of multisensory structured language education for student with dyslexia and related disorders* (pp. 16-19). Salem, OR: International Multisensory Structured Language Education Council.

Comenius, J. A. (1967). *The great didactic* (M. W. Keating, Trans.). New York: Russell & Russell. (Original work published 1632)

Connecticut State Department of Education. (1989). *A guide to the Connecticut School Effectiveness Project*. Middletown: Connecticut State Department of Education.

Council for Exceptional Children. (1996). *Principles for learning to read* [On-line]. Available: http://www.cec.sped/ericec/principle.htm

Daniels, H. (1996, Summer). Is whole language doomed? *The Voice: A Newsletter of the National Writing Project* [On-line]. Available: http://www-gse.berkeley.edu/research/NWP/Voice/sum96/sum96pg9.html

Darmer, M. (1995). *Developing transfer and metacognition skills in educationally disadvantaged students: Effects of the Higher Order Thinking Skills (HOTS) program*. Unpublished dissertation, University of Arizona.

Deal, T. (1986). Educational change: Revival tent, Tinkertoys, jungle, or carnival. In A. Lieberman (Ed.), *Rethinking school improvement: Research, craft, and concept* (pp. 115-128). New York: Teachers College Press.

Diegmueller, K. (1995, June 14). California plotting new tack on language arts. *Education Week* [On-line]. Available in the Archives: http://www.edweek.org/

Diegmueller, K. (1996, March 20). The best of both worlds. *Education Week,* pp. 32-33.

Duff, C. (1996, October 10). How whole language became a hot potato in and out of academia. *Wall Street Journal,* pp. A-1, A-9, A-10.

Edmonds, R. (1979). Effective schools for the urban poor. *Educational Leadership, 37*(1), 15-24.

Edmonds, R. (1981). Making public schools effective. *Social Policy, 12,* 53-60.

Ehri, L. C. (1986). Sources of difficulty in learning to spell and read. In M. L. Wolraich & D. Routh (Eds.), *Advances in developmental and behavioral pediatrics* (Vol. 7, pp. 121-195). Greenwich, CT: JAI.

Ellis, W. (1993). Through the barricades: Multisensory approaches. *Perspectives: The Orton Dyslexia Society, 19*(2), 7-12.

Emmer, E. T., & Everson, C. M. (1981). *Effective management at the beginning of the school year in junior high classes* (Report No. 6108). Austin: University of Texas, Research and Development Center of Teacher Education.

Engelmann, S., & Bruner, E. C. (1983). *Reading Mastery I and II: DISTAR reading.* Chicago: Science Research Associates.

Evertson, C. M. (1982). Differences in instructional activities in higher and lower achieving junior high English and mathematics classrooms. *Elementary School Journal, 82,* 329-351.

Farnham-Diggory, S. (1987, July). *From theory to practice in reading.* Paper presented at the annual meeting of the Reading Reform Foundation, San Francisco.

Feinberg, L. (1990). Multiple-choice and its critics. *College Board Review, 156,* 12-17.

Flesch, R. (1955). *Why Johnny can't read.* New York: Harper & Row.

Flesch, R. (1981). *Why Johnny still can't read: A new look at the scandal of our schools.* New York: Harper & Row.

Foorman, B., Francis, D., Beeler, T., Winikates, D., & Fletcher, J. (in press). Early interventions for children with reading problems: Study designs and preliminary findings. *Learning Disabilities: A Multi-Disciplinary Journal.*

Foorman, B., Francis, D., Novy, D., & Liberman, D. (1991). How letter-sound instruction mediates progress in first-grade reading and spelling. *Journal of Educational Psychology, 83,* 456-469.

Freedom Party of Ontario. (1997). *Whole language aliases* [On-line]. Available: http://www.freedomparty.org/wholmain.htm

Fullan, M. G. (1992). Visions that blind. *Educational Leadership, 49,* 19-20.

Gaskins, I. W., & Elliot, T. T. (with others). (1991). *Implementing cognitive strategy instruction across the school: The benchmark manual for teachers.* Cambridge, MA: Brookline Books.

Gauthier, W. (1980, October). Focusing for effectiveness. *Choices,* pp. 16-17.

Glass, G., & Camilli, G. (1981). *"Follow Through" evaluation.* Washington, DC: National Institute of Education. (ERIC Document Reproduction Service No. ED 244 738)

Goldring, E. B., & Rallis, S. F. (1993). *Principals of dynamic schools: Taking charge of change.* Newbury Park, CA: Corwin.

Goodman, K. (1986). *What's whole in whole language?* Exeter, NH: Heinemann.

Goodman, K. (1993). *Phonics phacts.* New York: Scholastic Press.

Goodman, K. (1995, November 15). Forced choices in a non-crisis: A critique of the report of the California Reading Task Force. *Education Week,* pp. 39, 42.

Gough, P. B., & Hillinger, M. L. (1980). Learning to read: An unnatural act. *Bulletin of the Orton Society, 30,* 179-196.

Gough, P. B., Hoover W. A., & Peterson, C. L. (1996). Some observations on a simple view of reading. In E. Cornoldi & J. Oakhill (Eds.), *Reading comprehension difficulties* (pp. 1-13). Mahwah, NJ: Lawrence Erlbaum.

Gough, P. B., Larson, K. C., & Yopp, H. (1997). *The structure of phonemic awareness* [On-line]. Available: http://www.psy.utexas.edu/psy/klarson/recife.html

Gray, W. S. (1960). *On their own in reading* (2nd ed.). Chicago: Scott, Foresman. (Original work published 1948)

Greer, C. (1995, May 28). When you read to a child, everybody wins. *Parade Magazine,* pp. 20-21.

Groff, P. (1991). Teachers' opinions of the whole language approach to reading instruction. *Annals of Dyslexia, 41,* 83-95.

Grossen, B. (1996). *30 years of research: What we now know about how children learn to read* [On-line]. Santa Cruz, CA: Center for the Future of Teaching and Learning. Available: http://www.cftl.org/reading.html

Grossen, B., Coulter, G., & Ruggles, B. (1996, Summer). Reading Recovery: An evaluation of benefits and costs. *Effective School Practices, 15*(3), 6-24.

Gurren, L., & Hughes, A. (1965). Intensive phonics vs. gradual phonics in beginning reading. *A Review Journal of Educational Research, 58,* 339-346.

Hallinger, P., Bickman, L., & Davis, K. (1996). School context, principal leadership, and student reading achievement. *Elementary School Journal, 96,* 527-549.

Harrison, C. R., Killion, J. P., & Mitchell, J. E. (1989). Site-based management: The realities of implementation. *Educational Leadership, 46*(8), 55-58.

Heck, R., Larson, T., & Marcoulides, G. (1990). Principal instructional leadership and school achievement: Validation of a causal model. *Educational Administration Quarterly, 26,* 94-125.

Heck, R., Marcoulides, G., & Lang, P. (1991). Principal instructional leadership and school achievement: The application of discriminant techniques. *School Effectiveness and School Improvement, 2,* 115-135.

Helmer, O. (1981, May). Interview: Olaf Helmer. *Omni,* pp. 81-84, 90.

Hiebert, E. (1994). Reading Recovery in the United States: What difference does it make to an age cohort? *Educational Researcher, 23*(9), 15-25.

Hirsch, E. D. (1987). *Cultural literacy.* Boston: Houghton Mifflin.

Hirsch, E. D. (1996). *The schools we need and why we don't have them.* New York: Doubleday.

Honig, B. (1996). *Teaching our children to read: The role of skills in a comprehensive reading program.* Thousand Oaks, CA: Corwin.

Huey, E. B. (1908). *The psychology and pedagogy of reading.* New York: Macmillan.

Johnson, T. D., & Louis, D. R. (1987). *Literacy through literature.* Portsmouth, NH: Heinemann.

Jones, B. F., Palincsar, A. S., Ogle, D. S., & Carr, E. G. (Eds.). (1987). *Strategic teaching and learning: Cognitive instruction in the content areas.* Alexandria, VA: Association for Supervision and Curriculum Development.

Juel, C., & Roper/Schneider, D. (1985). The influence of basals on first grade reading. *Reading Research Quarterly, 20,* 134-152.

Kentucky Department of Education. (1997). *Results-based practices showcase.* Frankfort: Kentucky Department of Education, School Improvement Division.

Lally, K., & Price, D. M. (1997, November 3). The brain reads sound by sound. *Baltimore Sun* [On-line]. Available: http://www.sunspot.net/

Latham, G. (1988, September). The birth and death cycles of educational innovations. *Principal,* pp. 41-43.

Lawton, M. (1997, November 26). Kentucky to showcase performance-linked curricula. *Education Week* [On-line]. Available: http://www.edweek.org/

Lehr, S. S. (1991). *The child's developing sense of theme: Responses to literature.* New York: Teachers College Press.

Lemann, N. (1997, November). The reading wars. *Atlantic Monthly,* pp. 128-134.

Levine, A. (1994, December). The great debate revisited. *Atlantic Monthly,* pp. 38-44.

Libit, H., & Bowler, M. (1997, November 3). The California story: A very costly lesson. *Baltimore Sun* [On-line]. Available: http://www.sunspot.net/

Lindamood, P., Bell, N., & Lindamood, P. (1997). Sensory-cognitive factors in the controversy over reading instruction. *Journal of Developmental and Learning Disorders, 1,* 143-182.

Lindamood-Bell Learning Processes. (1997). *Implementing the intensive clinic: A human learning management approach in an Alaska school district.* San Luis Obispo, CA: Author.

Lortie, D. (1975). *Schoolteacher.* Chicago: University of Chicago Press.

Louis, K., & Miles, M. (1990). *Improving the urban high school.* New York: Teachers College Press.

Lowell, J. R. (1871). *Books and libraries and other papers.* Boston: Houghton Mifflin.

Lukhele, R., Thissen, D., & Wainer, H. (1994). On the relative values of multiple-choice, constructed response, and examinee-selected items on two achievement tests. *Journal of Educational Measurement, 31*(3), 234-250.

Lynch, R. F., & Werner, T. J. (1992). *Continuous improvement: Teams and tools.* Atlanta, GA: QualTeam.

Lyon, R. (1997, April 23). Houston phonics study: A response to criticism [Letter to the editor]. *Education Week,* p. 50.

Machiavelli, N. (1985). *The prince* (H. C. Mansfield, Jr., Trans.). Chicago: University of Chicago Press.

Manzo, K. K. (1997a, January 15). Calif. text adoption puts emphasis on phonics. *Education Week* [On-line]. Available in the Archives: http://www.edweek.org/

Manzo, K. K. (1997b, March 12). Study stresses role of early phonics instruction. *Education Week,* p. 1.

Margosein, C. M., Pascarella, E. T., & Pflaum, S. W. (1982, April). *The effect of instruction using semantic mapping on vocabulary and comprehension.* Paper presented at the annual meeting of the American Educational Research Association, New York.

Martinez, P. (1997, February 16). Universities' reading ethos shuns extremes. *Arizona Daily Star,* Sec. A, p. 11.

Mathews, M. (1966). *Teaching to read, historically considered.* Chicago: University of Chicago Press.

McEwan, E. K. (1988). *The art of instructional leadership. Administrators' Academy for the Illinois State Board of Education.* Wheaton, IL: Educational Service Region for DuPage County.

McEwan, E. K. (1991a). *The best defense.* Joshua McIntire Series for Middle Grade Readers. Elgin, IL: David C. Cook.

McEwan, E. K. (1991b). *Project Cockroach.* Joshua McIntire Series for Middle Grade Readers. Elgin, IL: David C. Cook.

McEwan, E. K. (1993a). *Operation Garbage.* Joshua McIntire Series for Middle Grade Readers. Elgin, IL: David C. Cook.

McEwan, E. K. (1993b). *Underground hero.* Joshua McIntire Series for Middle Grade Readers. Elgin, IL: David C. Cook.

McEwan, E. K. (1994). *Murphy's mansion.* Joshua McIntire Series for Middle Grade Readers. Elgin, IL: David C. Cook.

McEwan, E. K. (1997a). *Leading your team to excellence: How to make quality decisions.* Thousand Oaks, CA: Corwin.

McEwan, E. K. (1997b). *Seven steps to effective instructional leadership.* Thousand Oaks, CA: Corwin.

McEwan, E. K. (in press). *How to raise a reader* (Rev. ed.). Grand Rapids, MI: Baker Book House.

McGuinness, C., McGuinness, D., & McGuinness, G. (1996). Phono-Graphix: A new method for remediating reading difficulties. *Orton Annals of Dyslexia, 46,* 73-96.

McGuinness, C., & McGuinness, G. (1998). *Reading reflex.* New York: Free Press.

McGuinness, D. (1997). *Why our children can't read and what we can do about it: A scientific revolution in reading.* New York: Free Press.

McIntyre, C. W., & Pickering, J. S. (Eds.). (1995). *Clinical studies of multisensory structured language education for students with dyslexia and related disorders.* Salem, OR: International Multisensory Structured Language Education Council.

McPike, E. (1995, Summer). Learning to read: Schooling's first mission. *American Educator,* pp. 3-6.

Meek, M. (1983). *Achieving literacy.* London: Routledge & Kegan Paul.

Mitchell, J. (Ed.). (1977). Phoenicia. In *Random House encyclopedia.* New York: Random House.

National Academy of Education, Commission on Reading. (1985). *Becoming a nation of readers: The report of the Commission on Reading* (Prepared by R. C. Anderson, E. H. Hiebert, J. A. Scott, & I. A. G. Wilkinson). Washington, DC: National Academy of Education, National Institute of Education, Center for the Study of Reading.

National Adult Literacy Survey. (1994). [On-line]. Available: http://www.ed.gov/pubs/ncesprograms/assessment/surveys/nals.html

National Center to Improve the Tools of Educators. (1997a). *A handbook for creating smart schools* [On-line]. Available: http://darkwing.uoregon.edu/ncite/smart.htm

National Center to Improve the Tools of Educators. (1997b). *Technical reports numbers 13-23: Synthesis of research and instructional implications for diverse learners* [On-line]. Available: http://darkwing.uoregon.edu/ncite/reading

Nevo, D. (1991, October). *An evaluation-minded school: Developing internal school evaluation systems.* Paper presented at the annual meeting of the American Evaluation Association, Chicago.

North, M. (1995). The effects of Spalding instruction on special education students. In C. W. McIntyre & J. S. Pickering (Eds.), *Clinical studies of multisensory structured language education for student with dyslexia and related disorders* (pp. 217-224). Salem, OR: International Multisensory Structured Language Education Council.

Northwest Regional Educational Laboratory. (1984). *Effective schooling practices: A research synthesis.* Portland, OR: Author.

Office of Educational Research and Improvement, U.S. Department of Education. (1996). *NAEP 1994. Reading report card for the nation and states.* Washington, DC: U.S. Department of Education.

Ogle, D. M. (1986). K-W-L: A teaching model that develops active reading of expository text. *Reading Teacher, 39,* 564-570.

Open Court Reading Series. (1997). De Soto, TX: SRA/McGraw-Hill.

Orton, S. T. (1989). *Reading, writing, and speech problems in children and selected papers.* Austin, TX: Pro-Ed. (Original work published 1937)

Palincsar, A. M., & Brown, A. L. (1984). Reciprocal teaching of comprehension fostering and comprehension monitoring activities. *Cognition and Instruction, 1,* 117-175.

Palmaffy, T. (1997, November). See Dick flunk. *Policy Review* [On-line]. Available: http://www.policyreview.com/heritage/p_review/nov97/flun

Parker, G. M. (1990). *Team players and teamwork.* San Francisco: Jossey-Bass.

Pearson, P. D. (1993, October). Teaching and learning reading: A research perspective. *Language Arts, 70,* 502-511.

Pearson, P. D., & Dole, S. (1987). Explicit comprehension instruction: A review of research and a new conceptualization of instruction. *Elementary School Journal, 88,* 151-165.

Phi Delta Kappa. (1980). *Why do some urban schools succeed?* Bloomington, IN: Author.

Pinnell, G. S., & Lyons, C. (1995). *Response to Hiebert: What difference does Reading Recovery make?* Unpublished manuscript.

Pinnell, S. G., Lyons, C. A., & DeFord, D. E. (1988). *Reading Recovery: Early intervention for at-risk first graders.* Arlington, VA: Educational Research Service.

Pogrow, S. (1995). *A revalidation of the effectiveness of the HOTS program prepared for the National Diffusion Network.* Unpublished paper.

Pogrow, S. (1997). Using technology to combine process and content. In A. Costa & R. Liebman (Eds.), *Supporting the spirit of learning: When process is content* (pp. 99-116). Thousand Oaks, CA: Corwin.

Popp, H. M. (1975). Current practices in the teaching of beginning reading. In J. B. Carroll & J. S. Chall (Eds.), *Toward a literate society: The report of the Committee on Reading of the National Academy of Education.* New York: McGraw-Hill.

Pressley, M. (1991). Strategy instruction at Benchmark School: A faculty interview study. *Learning Disabilities Quarterly, 14*(1), 19-48.

Pressley, M., Woloshyn, V., & Associates. (1995). *Cognitive strategy instruction that really improves children's academic performance.* Cambridge, MA: Brookline Books.

Purkey, S., & Smith, M. (1983). Research on effective schools: A review. *Elementary School Journal, 83*(4), 427-452.

Rosenshine, B. (1983). Teaching functions in instructional programs. *Elementary School Journal, 83*(4), 335-351.

Rossi, R. (1997, September 8). Reading scores tumble. *Chicago Sun-Times,* Sec. 1, pp. 1-2.

Routman, R. (1996). *Literacy at the crossroads: Crucial talk about reading, writing, and other teaching dilemmas.* Portsmouth, NH: Heinemann.

Rutter, M., Maughan, B., Mortimore, P., & Ouston, J. (1979). *Fifteen thousand hours.* Cambridge, MA: Harvard University Press.

Sanders, W., & Rivers, J. C. (1996, November). *Cumulative and residual effects of teachers on future student academic achievement.* Knoxville: University of Tennessee Value Added Research and Assessment Center.

Sarason, S. (1990). *The predictable future of educational reform: Can we change course before it's too late?* San Francisco: Jossey-Bass.

Schuder, T. (1993). The genesis of transactional strategies instruction in a reading program for at-risk students. *Elementary School Journal, 94,* 183-200.

Scriven, M. (1967). The methodology of evaluation. In R. W. Tyler, R. M. Gagne, & M. Scriven (Eds.), *Perspectives of curriculum evaluation* (AERA Monograph Series on Curriculum Evaluation No. 1, pp. 39-82). Chicago: Rand McNally.

Shany, M. T., & Biemiller, A. (1995). Assisted reading practice: Effects on performance for poor readers in Grades 3 & 4. *Reading Research Quarterly, 50,* 382-395.

Share, D. L. (1995). Phonological recoding and self-teaching: Sine qua non of reading acquisition. *Cognition: International Journal of Cognitive Science, 55,* 151-218.

Share, D. L., & Stanovich, K. E. (1995). Cognitive processes in early reading development: Accommodating individual differences into a mode of acquisition. *Issues in Education: Contributions From Educational Psychology, 1,* 1-57.

Short, E. J., & Ryan, E. B. (1984). Metacognitive differences between skilled and less skilled readers: Remediating deficits through story grammar and attribution training. *Journal of Educational Psychology, 76,* 225-235.

Shu, H., Anderson, R., & Shang, H. (1995). Incidental learning of word meanings while reading. *Reading Research Quarterly, 30,* 76-86.

Siegel, J. (1997, October 8). Jewel in the crown. *Education Week,* pp. 24-29.

Sillins, H. (1994). The relationship between school leadership and school improvement outcomes. *School Effectiveness and School Improvement, 5,* 272-298.

Slavin, R. E., & Madden, N. A. (1995, April). *Effects of Success for All on the achievement of English language learners.* Paper presented at the annual meeting of the American Educational Research Association, San Francisco.

Slavin, R. E., Madden, N. A., Dolan, L. J., & Wasik, B. A. (1996). *Every child, every school: Success for all.* Thousand Oaks, CA: Corwin.

Smith, F. (1973). *Psychology and reading.* New York: Holt, Rinehart & Winston.

Smith, F. (1985a). *Reading.* New York: Cambridge University Press.

Smith, F. (1985b). *Reading without nonsense: Making sense of reading.* New York: Teachers College Press.

Smith, F. (1986). *Understanding reading.* Hillsdale, NJ: Lawrence Erlbaum.

Smith, F. (1994). *Understanding reading: A psycholinguistic analysis of reading and learning to read* (5th ed.). Hillsdale, NJ: Lawrence Erlbaum.

Spagnolo, J. (1997, November 2). Gift of reading [Letter to the editor]. *Daily Herald,* Sec. 1, p. 17.

Spalding, R. B., & Spalding, W. T. (1990). *The writing road to reading: The Spalding method of phonics for teaching speech, writing & reading* (4th ed., rev.). New York: William Morrow. (Original work published 1957)

Spear-Swerling, L., & Sternberg, R. (1996). *Off track.* Boulder, CO: Westview.

Stahl, S. (1995). Does whole language or instruction matched to learning styles help children learn to read? *School Psychology Review, 24,* 393-405.

Stallings, J. (1979). *How to change the process of teaching basic reading skills in secondary schools: Executive summary.* Menlo Park, CA: SRI International.

Stallings, J. (1980). Allocated academic learning time revisited, or beyond time on task. *Educational Researcher, 9,* 11-16.

Stanovich, K. E. (1986). Matthew effects in reading: Some consequences of individual differences in the acquisition of literacy. *Reading Research Quarterly, 21,* 360-407.

Stanovich, K. E. (1993). Does reading make you smarter? Literacy and the development of verbal intelligence. In H. Reese (Ed.), *Advances in child development and behavior* (Vol. 25, pp. 133-180). San Diego, CA: Academic Press.

Stanovich, K. E. (1994). Romance and reality. *The Reading Teacher, 47*(4), 280-291.

Stebbins, L. B., St. Pierre, R. G., & Proper, E. C. (1977). *Education as experimentation: A planned variation model: Vol. IV, A & B. Effects of Follow Through models.* Cambridge, MA: Abt.

Texas Alternative Document. (1997). *Texas essential knowledge and skills: Texas alternative document: English/language arts/reading* [On-line]. Available: http://www.htcomp.net/tad

Torgesen, J. K. (in press). Instructional interventions for children with reading disabilities. In G. Shapiro, D. Accardi, & I. Caputi (Eds.), *Dyslexia: Conceptualization, diagnosis, and treatment.* Parkton, MD: York Press.

Torgesen, J. K., Wagner, R., Rashotte, C. A., Alexander, A. W., & Conway, T. (in press). Preventive and remedial interventions for children with severe reading disabilities. *Learning Disabilities: A Multidisciplinary Journal.*

Treddlie, C., Kirby, P. C., & Stringfield, S. (1989). Effective versus ineffective schools: Observable differences in the classroom. *American Journal of Education, 97,* 221-236.

Venezky, R. L., & Winfield, L. F. (1979). *Schools that succeed beyond expectations in reading* (Studies in Education). Newark: University of Delaware. (ERIC Document Reproduction Service No. ED 177 484)

Wasik, B. A., & Slavin, R. E. (1993). Preventing early reading failure with one-to-one tutoring: A review of five programs. *Reading Research Quarterly, 28,* 179-200.

Weaver, C. (1980). *Psycholinguistics and reading.* Cambridge, MA: Winthrop.

Weaver, C. (1988). *Reading process and practice.* Exeter, NH: Heinemann.

Index

CORWIN
PRESS

The Corwin Press logo—a raven striding across an open book—represents the happy union of courage and learning. We are a professional-level publisher of books and journals for K-12 educators, and we are committed to creating and providing resources that embody these qualities. Corwin's motto is "Success for All Learners."